MW00710641

The sermons of Mr. Yorick. ... A new edition. Volume 2 of 2

Laurence Sterne

The sermons of Mr. Yorick. ... A new edition. Volume 2 of 2
Sterne, Laurence
ESTCID: T207267
Reproduction from John Rylands University Library of Manchester
Mr. Yorick = Laurence Sterne.
London : sold by R. Dampier, J. Thompson, W. Manson, T. Davidson, and P. Watson, [1790?].
2v. ; 12°

Eighteenth Century
Collections Online
Print Editions

Gale ECCO Print Editions

Relive history with *Eighteenth Century Collections Online*, now available in print for the independent historian and collector. This series includes the most significant English-language and foreign-language works printed in Great Britain during the eighteenth century, and is organized in seven different subject areas including literature and language; medicine, science, and technology; and religion and philosophy. The collection also includes thousands of important works from the Americas.

The eighteenth century has been called "The Age of Enlightenment." It was a period of rapid advance in print culture and publishing, in world exploration, and in the rapid growth of science and technology – all of which had a profound impact on the political and cultural landscape. At the end of the century the American Revolution, French Revolution and Industrial Revolution, perhaps three of the most significant events in modern history, set in motion developments that eventually dominated world political, economic, and social life.

In a groundbreaking effort, Gale initiated a revolution of its own: digitization of epic proportions to preserve these invaluable works in the largest online archive of its kind. Contributions from major world libraries constitute over 175,000 original printed works. Scanned images of the actual pages, rather than transcriptions, recreate the works *as they first appeared.*

Now for the first time, these high-quality digital scans of original works are available via print-on-demand, making them readily accessible to libraries, students, independent scholars, and readers of all ages.

For our initial release we have created seven robust collections to form one the world's most comprehensive catalogs of 18th century works.

Initial Gale ECCO Print Editions collections include:

History and Geography
Rich in titles on English life and social history, this collection spans the world as it was known to eighteenth-century historians and explorers. Titles include a wealth of travel accounts and diaries, histories of nations from throughout the world, and maps and charts of a world that was still being discovered. Students of the War of American Independence will find fascinating accounts from the British side of conflict.

Social Science

Delve into what it was like to live during the eighteenth century by reading the first-hand accounts of everyday people, including city dwellers and farmers, businessmen and bankers, artisans and merchants, artists and their patrons, politicians and their constituents. Original texts make the American, French, and Industrial revolutions vividly contemporary.

Medicine, Science and Technology

Medical theory and practice of the 1700s developed rapidly, as is evidenced by the extensive collection, which includes descriptions of diseases, their conditions, and treatments. Books on science and technology, agriculture, military technology, natural philosophy, even cookbooks, are all contained here.

Literature and Language

Western literary study flows out of eighteenth-century works by Alexander Pope, Daniel Defoe, Henry Fielding, Frances Burney, Denis Diderot, Johann Gottfried Herder, Johann Wolfgang von Goethe, and others. Experience the birth of the modern novel, or compare the development of language using dictionaries and grammar discourses.

Religion and Philosophy

The Age of Enlightenment profoundly enriched religious and philosophical understanding and continues to influence present-day thinking. Works collected here include masterpieces by David Hume, Immanuel Kant, and Jean-Jacques Rousseau, as well as religious sermons and moral debates on the issues of the day, such as the slave trade. The Age of Reason saw conflict between Protestantism and Catholicism transformed into one between faith and logic -- a debate that continues in the twenty-first century.

Law and Reference

This collection reveals the history of English common law and Empire law in a vastly changing world of British expansion. Dominating the legal field is the *Commentaries of the Law of England* by Sir William Blackstone, which first appeared in 1765. Reference works such as almanacs and catalogues continue to educate us by revealing the day-to-day workings of society.

Fine Arts

The eighteenth-century fascination with Greek and Roman antiquity followed the systematic excavation of the ruins at Pompeii and Herculaneum in southern Italy; and after 1750 a neoclassical style dominated all artistic fields. The titles here trace developments in mostly English-language works on painting, sculpture, architecture, music, theater, and other disciplines. Instructional works on musical instruments, catalogs of art objects, comic operas, and more are also included.

old books. new life.

The BiblioLife Network

This project was made possible in part by the BiblioLife Network (BLN), a project aimed at addressing some of the huge challenges facing book preservationists around the world. The BLN includes libraries, library networks, archives, subject matter experts, online communities and library service providers. We believe every book ever published should be available as a high-quality print reproduction; printed on-demand anywhere in the world. This insures the ongoing accessibility of the content and helps generate sustainable revenue for the libraries and organizations that work to preserve these important materials.

The following book is in the "public domain" and represents an authentic reproduction of the text as printed by the original publisher. While we have attempted to accurately maintain the integrity of the original work, there are sometimes problems with the original work or the micro-film from which the books were digitized. This can result in minor errors in reproduction. Possible imperfections include missing and blurred pages, poor pictures, markings and other reproduction issues beyond our control. Because this work is culturally important, we have made it available as part of our commitment to protecting, preserving, and promoting the world's literature.

GUIDE TO FOLD-OUTS MAPS and OVERSIZED IMAGES

The book you are reading was digitized from microfilm captured over the past thirty to forty years. Years after the creation of the original microfilm, the book was converted to digital files and made available in an online database.

In an online database, page images do not need to conform to the size restrictions found in a printed book. When converting these images back into a printed bound book, the page sizes are standardized in ways that maintain the detail of the original. For large images, such as fold-out maps, the original page image is split into two or more pages

Guidelines used to determine how to split the page image follows:

• Some images are split vertically; large images require vertical and horizontal splits.
• For horizontal splits, the content is split left to right.
• For vertical splits, the content is split from top to bottom.
• For both vertical and horizontal splits, the image is processed from top left to bottom right.

THE
SERMONS
OF
Mr. YORICK.

VOL. II.

A NEW EDITION.

LONDON.

Sold by R DAMPIER J THOMPSON, W
MANSON, T. DAVIDSON, and P.
WATSON.

SERMONS

BY

LAURENCE STERNE,
A. M. Prebendary of York, and
Vicar of Sutton on the Foreſt, and
of Stillington near York.

VOL. II.

A 2

SERMONS

BY

LAURENCE STERNE,
A. M. Prebendary of York, and Vicar of Sutton on the Foreſt, and of Stillington near York.

VOL. II.

SERMON VIII.

TIME and CHANCE.

SERMON VIII.

ECCLESIASTES ix. 11.

I returned and saw under the sun, that the race is not to the swift,---nor the battle to the strong,---neither yet bread to the wise, nor yet riches to men of understanding, nor yet favour to men of skill,---but time and chance happeneth to them all.

WHEN a man casts a look upon this melancholy description of the world, and sees contrary to all his guesses and expectations, what different fates attend the lives of men,---how oft it happens in the world, that there is not even bread to the wise, nor riches to men of

A 4   understanding,

underftanding, &c.——he is apt to
conclude with a figh upon it,——in
the words,——though not in the fenfe
of the wife man,——that time and
chance happeneth to them all ---That
time and chance,——apt feafons and
fit conjunctures have the greateft
away, in the turns and difpofals of
men's fortunes.   And that, as thefe
lucky hits, (as they are called) hap-
pen to be for, or againft a man,---
they either open the way to his advancement againft all obftacles,——
or block it up againft all helps and
attempts.   That as the text inti-
mates, neither *wifdom,* nor *under-
ftanding,* nor *fkill* fhall be able to fur-
mount them.

However widely we may differ in
our reafonings upon this obfervation
of Solomon's, the authority of the
obfervation

obfervation is ftrong beyond doubt, and the evidence given of it in all a-ges fo alternately confirmed by examples and complaints, as to leave the fact itfelf unqueftionable.—That things are carried on in this world, fometimes fo contrary to all our rea-fonings, and the feeming probabili-ties of fuccefs,---that, even the race is not to the fwift, nor the battle to the ftrong,---nay, what is ftranger ftill——nor yet bread to the wife, who fhould laft ftand in want of it, ---nor yet riches to men of under-ftanding, who you would think beft qualified to acquire them,---nor yet favour to men of fkill, whofe merit and pretences bid the faireft for it, ---but that there are fome fecret and unfeen workings in human affairs, which baffle all our endeavours,---' and turn afide the courfe of things in fuch a manner,——that the moſt likely cauſes diſappoint and fail of producing for us the effect which we wiſhed and naturally expected from them.

You will ſee a man, of whom was you to form a conjecture from the appearances of things in his favour, ——you would ſay was ſetting out in the world, with the faireſt proſpect of making his fortune in it ;——with all the advantages of birth to recommend him,————of perſonal merit to ſpeak for him,——and of friends to help and puſh him forwards : you will behold him, notwithſtanding this, diſappointed in every effect you might naturally have looked for from them ; every ſtep he takes towards his advancement, ſomething inviſible ſhall pull him back, ſome

unforeſeen

unforefeen obftacle fhall rife up perpetually in his way, and keep there.
———In every application he makes,
—fome untoward circumftance fhall
blaft it.———He fhall rife early,—
late take reft,———and eat the bread
of carefulnefs,—yet fome happier
man fhall ftill rife up, and ever ftep
in before him, and leave him ftruggling to the end of his life, in the
very fame place, in which he firft
begun it.

THE hiftory of a fecond, fhall in
all refpects be the contraft to this.
He fhall come into the world with
the moft unpromifing appearance,—
fhall fet forwards without fortune,
without friends,—without talents to
procure him either the one or the o-
ther. Neverthelefs, you will fee this
clouded profpect brighten up infen-

fibly, unaccountably before him ; every thing prefented in his way, fhall turn out beyond his expectations,---in fpight of that chain of unfurmountable difficulties which firft threatened him,---time and chance fhall open him a way,---a feries of fuccefsful occurrences fhall lead him by the hand to the fummit of honour and fortune, and in a word, without giving him the pains of thinking, or the credit of projecting it, fhall place him in fafe poffeffion of all that ambition could wifh for.

THE hiftories of the lives and fortunes of men are full of inftances of this nature,---where favourable times and lucky accidents have done for them, what wifdom or fkill could not: and there is fcarce any one who has lived long in the world, who,

upon

upon looking backwards, will not difcover fuch a mixture of thefe in the many fuccefsful turns which have. happened in his life, as to leave him very little reafon to difpute againft the fact, and, I fhould hope, as little upon the conclufions to be drawn from it.

Some, indeed, from a fuperficial view of this reprefentation of things, have atheiftically inferred,——that becaufe there was fo much of lottery in this life,——and mere cafualty feemed to have fuch a fhare in the difpofal of our affairs,——that the providence of God ftood neuter and unconcerned in their feveral workings, leaving them to the mercy of time and chance, to be furthered or difappointed as fuch blind agents directed. Whereas in truth the very oppofite

oppofite conclufion follows. For confider,——if a fuperior intelligent power did not fometimes crofs and over-rule events in this world,—— then our policies and defigns in it, would always anfwer according to the wifdom and ftratagem in which they were laid, and every caufe, in the courfe of things, would produce its natural effect without variation. Now as this is not the cafe, it neceffarily follows from Solomon's reafoning, that, if the race is not to the fwift, if knowledge and learning do not always fecure men from want, ——nor care and induftry always make men rich,——nor art and fkill infallibly make men high in the world; that there is fome other caufe which mingles itfelf in human affairs, and governs and turns them as it pleafes; which caufe can be no other than the

the firſt cauſe of all things, and the ſecret and over-ruling providence of that Almighty God, who though his dwelling is ſo high, yet he humbleth himſelf to behold the things that are done in earth, raiſing up the poor out of the duſt, and lifting the beggar from the dunghill, and contrary to all hopes putting him with princes, even with the princes of his people; which by the way, was the caſe of David, who makes the acknowledgment [1]---And no doubt---one reaſon, why God has ſelected to his own diſpoſal, ſo many inſtances as this, where events have run counter to all probabilities,——was to give teſtimony to his providence in governing the world, and to engage us to a conſideration and dependence upon it, for the event and ſucceſs

of

of our undertakings *. For un-
doubtedly---as I said,---it should seem
but suitable to nature's law, that the
race should ever be to the swift,-----
and the battle to the strong;-----it is
reasonable that the best contrivances
and means should have best success,
-----and since it often falls out other-
wise in the case of man, where the
wisest projects are overthrown,------
and the most hopeful means are blasted, and time and chance happens to
all;---You must call in the Deity to
untie this knot,---for though at sun-
dry times---sundry events fall out,
which we who look no further than
the events themselves, call chance,
because they fall out quite contrary
both to our intentions and our hopes,
-----though at the same time, in respect of God's providence over-ruling

* Vid Tillotson's sermon on this subject.

ling in thefe events ; it were piofane to call them chance, for they are puie defignation, and though invifible, arc ftill the regular difpenfations of the fupeiintending power of that Almighty being, from whom all the laws and poweis of nature are derived,---who, as he has appointed, ---fo holds them as inftruments in his hands : and without invading the liberty and free-will of his creatures, can turn the paffions and defires of their hearts to fulfil his own righteoufnefs, and work fuch effects in human affairs, which to us feem merely *cafual*,——but to him, certain and determined, and what his infinite wifdom fees neceffary to be brought about for the government, and prefervation of the world, over which providence perpetually prefides.

WHEN

WHEN the fons of Jacob had caſt their brother Joſeph into the pit for his deſtruction,---one would think, if ever any incident which concern-ed the life of man deſerved to be call-ed chance, it was this.---That the company of Iſhmaelites-ſhould hap-pen to paſs by, in that open coun-try, at that very place, at that time too, when this barbarity was com-mitted. After he was reſcued by ſo favourable a contingency,---his life and future fortune ſtill depended up-on a ſeries of contingencies equally improbable; for inſtance, had the buſineſs of the Iſhmaelites who brought him, carried them from Gi-lead, to any other part of the world beſides Egypt, or when they arrived there, had they ſold their bond-flave to any other man but Potiphar, throughout the whole empire,——

or, after that difposal, had the unjuft accufations of his mafter's wife
caft the youth into any other dun-
geon, than that where the king's
prifoners were kept,---or had it fallen
out at any other crifis, than when
Pharaoh's chief butler was caft there
too,---had this, or any other of thefe
events fallen out otherwife than it
did,——a feries of unmerited misfortunes had overwhelmed him,———and
in confequence the whole land of E-
gypt and Canaan.   From the firft
opening, to the conclufion of this
long and interefting tranfaction, the
providence of God fuffered every
thing to take its courfe: the malice
and cruelty of Jofeph's brethren,
wrought their worft mifchief againft
him ;---banifhed him from his country and the protection of his parent.
—The luft and bafenefs of a difappointed

pointed woman funk him ftill deeper:——loaded his character with an unjuft reproach,——and to compleat his ruin, doomed him, friendlefs, to the miferies of a hopelefs prifon where he lay neglected. Providence, though it did not crofs thefe events,——yet Providence bent them to the moft merciful ends. When the whole DRAMA was opened, then the wifdom and contrivance of every part of it was difplayed. Then it appeared, it was not they (as the patriarch inferred in confolation of his brethren,) it was not they who fold him, but God,—'twas he fent him thither before them,—his fuperintending power availed itfelf of their paffions—directed the operations of them,—held the chain in his hand, and turned and wound it to his own purpofe. " Ye verily thought evil againft me,

but

—but God meant it for good,——ye
had the guilt of a bad intention,—
his providence the glory of accom-
plifhing a good one,——by prefer-
ving *you a pofterity upon the earth,*
and bring to pafs as it is this day,
to fave much people alive." All hiftory is full of fuch teftimonies, which
though they may convince thofe who
look no deeper than the furface of
things, that time and chance happen
to all,---yet to thofe who look deeper, they manifeft at the fame time,
that there is a hand much bufier in
human affairs than what we vainly
calculate; which though the pro-
jectors of this world overlook,———or
at leaft make no allowance for in the
formation of their plans, they generally find it in the execution of them.
And though the fatalift may urge,
that every event in this life, is brought
about

about by the miniftry and chain of natural caufes,---yet, in anfwer,--- let him go one ftep higher——and confider,——whofe power it is, that enables thefe caufes to work,---whofe knowledge it is, that forefees what will be their effects,——whofe good- nefs it is, that is invifibly conduct- ing them forwards to the beft and greateft ends for the happinefs of his creatures.

So that as a great reafoner juftly diftinguifhes, upon this point,---" It is not only, religioufly fpeaking, but with the ftricteft and moft philofo- phical truth of expreffion, that the fcripture tells us, *that* GOD *command-eth* the ravens,-----that they are his directions, which *the winds and the feas obey.* If his fervant hides him- felf by the brook, fuch an order,

caufes

caufes and effects fhall be laid,—that the fowls of the air fhall minifter to his fupport.----When this refource fails, and his prophet is directed to go to Zarepha,------for that he has *commanded* a widow woman there to fuftain him,-- the fame hand which leads the prophet to the gate of the city,---fhall lead forth the diftreffed widow to the fame place, to take him under her roof,---and though upon the impulfe of a different occafion, fhall neverthelefs be made to fulfil his promife and intention of their mutual prefervation."

THUS much for the truth and illuftration of this great and fundamental doctrine of a providence; the belief of which is of fuch confequence to us, as to be the great fupport and comfort of our lives.

JUSTLY

JUSTLY therefore might the Pfalmift upon this declaration,---that the Lord is King---conclude, that the earth may be glad therefore, yea the multitude of the ifles may be glad thereof.

MAY GOD grant the perfuafion may make us as virtuous, as it has reafon to make us joyful, and that it may bring forth in us the fruits of good living to his praife and glory, to whom be all might, majefty, and dominion, now and for evermore, *Amen.*

SERMON IX.

The Character of HEROD.

Preached on Innocents Day.

SERMON IX.

MATTHEW xi. 17. 18.

Then was fulfilled that which was fpo-
ken by Jeremy the prophet, faying,
——In Rama was there a voice
heard, lamentation, and weeping,
and great mourning, Rachael weep-
ing for her children, and would not
be comforted becaufe they are not.

THE words which St. Matthew
cites here as fulfilled by the
cruelty and ambition of Herod,---are
in the 31ft chapter of Jeremiah 15th
verfe. In the foregoing chapter,
the prophet having declared God's
intention of turning the mourning
of his people into joy, by the reftoration of the tribes which had been

B 2   led

led away captive into Babylon; he proceeds in the beginning of this chapter, which contains this prophecy, to give a more particular defcription of the great joy and feftivity of that promifed day, when they were to return once more to their own land, to enter upon their ancient poffeffions, and enjoy again all the privileges they had loft, and amongft others, and what was above them all,——the favour and protection of God, and the continuation of his mercies to them and their pofterity.

To make therefore the impreffion of this change the ftronger upon their minds—he gives a very pathetic reprefentation of the preceding forrow on that day when they were firft led away captive.

THUS

THUS faith the Lord, A voice was heard in Rama; lamentation and bitter weeping, Rachael weeping for her children, refufed to be comforted, becaufe they were not.

To enter into the full fenfe and beauty of this defcription, it is to be remembered that the tomb of Rachael, Jacob's beloved wife, as we read in the 35th of Genefis, was fituated near Rama, and betwixt that place and Bethlehem. Upon which circumftance the prophet raifes one of the moft affecting fcenes, that could be conceived; for as the tribes in their forrowful journey betwixt Rama and Bethlehem in their way to Babylon, were fuppofed to pafs by this monumental pillar of their anceftor Rachael, Jacob's wife, the prophet by a common liberty in rheto-

tic, introduces her as rifing up out
of her fepulchre, and as the common mother of two of their tribes,
weeping for her children, bewailing
the fad cataftrophe of her pofterity
led away into a ftrange land——refufing to be comforted becaufe they
were not,-----loft and cut off from
their country, and in all likelihood,
never to be reftored back to her a-
gain.

THE Jewifh interpreters fay upon
this, that the patriarch Jacob buried
Rachael in this very place, forfeeing
by the fpirit of prophecy, that, his
pofterity fhould that way be led captive, that fhe might as they paffed
her, intercede for them.------

BUT this fanciful fuperftructure
upon the paffage, feems to be little
elfe

elſe than a mere dream of ſome of the Jewiſh doctors ; and indeed had they not dreamt it when they did, 'tis great odds, but ſome of the Romiſh dreamers would have hit upon it before now. For, as it favours the doctrine of interceſſions—if there had not been undeniable vouchers for the real inventors of the conceit, one ſhould much ſooner have ſought for it amongſt the oral traditions of this church, than in the Talmud, where it is.——

But this by the bye. There is ſtill another interpretation of the words here cited by St. Matthew, which altogether excludes this ſcenecal repreſentation I have given of them.——By which 'tis thought that the lamentation of Rachael, here deſcribed, has no im-

mediate

mediate reference to Rachael, Jacob's wife, but that it simply alludes to the sorrows of her descendents, the distressed mothers of the tribes of Benjamin and Ephraim, who might accompany their children, led into captivity as far as Rama, in their way to Babylon, who wept and wailed upon this sad occasion, and as the prophet describes them in the person of Rachael, refusing to be comforted for the loss of her children, looking upon their departure without hope or prospect of ever beholding a return.

WHICH ever of the two senses you give the words of the prophet, the application of them by the evangelist is equally just and faithful. For as the former scene he relates, was transacted upon the very same stage,

in

—in the fame diftrict of Bethlehem
near Rama——where fo many mothers of the fame tribe now fuffered
this fecond moft affecting blow——
the words of Jeremiah, as the evangelift obferves, were literally accom-
plifhed, and no doubt, in that horrid day, a voice was heard again in
Rama, lamentation and bitter weep-
ing----Rachael weeping for her children, and refufing to be comforted;
——every Bethlemitifh mother involved in this calamity, beholding it
with hopelefs forrow gave vent to
it---each one, bewailing her children,
and lamenting the hardnefs of their
lot, with the anguifh of a heart as
incapable of confolation, as they were
of redrefs. Monfter!——could no
confideration of all this tender forrow
ftay thy hands?——Could no reflection upon fo much bitter lamentation

throughout

throughout the coafts of Bethlehem,
interpofe and plead in behalf of fo
many wretched objects, as this tragedy would make?—Was there no
way open to ambition but that thou
muft trample upon the affections of
nature? Could no pity for the innocence of childhood———no fympathy
for the yernings of parental love incline thee to fome other meafures for
thy fecurity—but thou muft thus
pitilefsly rufh in——take the victim
by violence—tear it from the em-
braces of the mother---offer it up before her eyes-----leave her difconfolate for ever---broken-hearted with a
lofs-----fo affecting in itfelf-----fo cir-
cumftanced with horror, that no time,
how friendly foever to the mournful
-----fhould ever be able to wear out
the impreffions?

THERE is nothing in which the
mind of man is more divided than
in the accounts of this horrid nature.
-----For when we confider man, as
fafhioned by his Maker---innocent
and upright---full of the tenderest
difpofitions---with a heart inclining
him to kindnefs, and the love and
protection of his fpecies---this idea of
him would almoft fhake the credit
of fuch accounts ;-----fo that to clear
them-----we are forced to take a fecond view of man-----very different
from this favourable one, in which
we infenfibly reprefent him to our i-
maginations---that is---we are obliged
to confider him------not as he was
made-----but as he is-----a creature by
the violence and irregularity of his
paffions capable of being perverted
from all thefe friendly and benevolent propenfities, and fometimes hur-

ried

ried into exceffes fo oppofite to them, as to render the moft unnatural and horrid accounts of what he does but too probable.---The truth of this obfervation will be exemplified in the cafe before us. For next to the faith and character of the hiftorian who reports fuch facts,-----the particular character of the perfon who committed them is to be confidered as a voucher for their truth and credibility ;---and if upon enquiry, it appears, that the man acted but confiftent with himfelf,-----and juft fo as you would have expected from his principles,---the credit of the hiftorian is reftored,---and the fact related ftands inconteftable, from fo ftrong and concurring an evidence on its fide.-----

WITH this view, it may not be
an

an unacceptable application of the re-
maining part of a difcourfe upon
this day, to give you a fketch of the
character of Herod, not as drawn
from fcripture,------for in general it
furnifhes us with few materials for
fuch defcriptions :---the facred fcripture cuts off in few words the hiftory of the ungodly, how great foever
they were in the eyes of the world,
------and on the other hand dwells
largely upon the. fmalleft actions of
the righteous.-----We find all the circumftances of the lives of Abraham,
Ifaac, Jacob and. Jofeph, recorded in
the minuteft manner.------The wicked
feem only mentioned with regret;
juft brought upon the ftage, on purpofe to be condemned. The ufe and
advantage of which conduct—is, I
fuppofe, the reafon,——as in general
it enlarges on no character, but what

is

is worthy of imitation. 'Tis however undeniable, that the lives of bad
men arc not without ufe,——and
whenever fuch a one is drawn, not
with a corrupt view to be admired,
---but on puipofe to be detefted,---it
muft excite fuch an horror againft
vice, as will ftrike indirectly the fame
good impreffion.   And though it is
painful to the laft degree to paint a
man in the fhades which his vices-
have caft upon him,---yet when it
ferves this end, and at the fame time
illuftrates a point in facred hiftory
------it carries its own excufe with
it.

THIS Herod, therefore, of whom
the evangelift fpeaks, if you take a
fuperficial view of his life, you would
fay was a compound of good and e-
vil,------that though he was certainly

ly a bad man,—yet you would think the mass was tempered at the same time with a mixture of good qualities. So that, in course, as is not uncommon, he would appear with two characters very different from each other. If you looked on the more favourable side, you would see a man of great address-----popular in his behaviour,—generous, prince-like in his entertainments and ex-pences, and in a word set off with all such virtue and shewy properties, as bid high for the countenance and approbation of the world.

VIEW him in another light, he was an ambitious, designing man, ------suspicious of all the world,---ra-pacious,---implacable in his temper, without sense of religion,---or feeling of humanity.------Now in all such

complex

complex characters as this,---the way
the world usually judges, is-----to sum
up the good and the bad against each
other.-----Deduct the lesser of these
articles from the greater, and (as we
do in passing other accounts) give
credit to the man for what remains
upon the balance.   Now, though
this seems a fair,-- --yet I fear, 'tis
often a fallacious reckoning,---which
though it may serve in many ordi-
nary cases of private life, yet will
not hold good in the more notorious instances of men's lives, espe-
cially when so complicated with good
and bad, as to exceed all common
bounds and proportions.   Not to be
deceived in such cases, we must work
by a different rule, which though it
may appear less candid,-----yet to
make amends, I am persuaded will
bring us in general much nearer to
the

the thing we want,-----which is truth.
The way to which is-----in all judg-
ments of this kind, to diftinguifh and
carry in your eye, the principle and
ruling paffion which leads the cha-
racter---and feparate that from the
other parts of it,-----and then take
notice, how far his other qualities,
good and bad, are brought to ferve
and fupport that. For want of this
diftinction, we often think ourfelves
inconfiftent creatures, when we are
the furtheft from it, and all the variety of fhapes and contradictory appearances we put on, are in truth
but fo many different attempts to gratify the fame governing appetite.----

WITH this clew, let us endeavour
to unravel this character of Herod as
here given.

THE firft thing which ftrikes one in it is ambition, an immoderate thirft, as well as jealoufy of power; -----how inconfiftent foever in other parts, his character appears invariable in this, and every action of his life was true to it.---From hence we may venture to conclude, that this was *his* ruling paffion,-----and that moft, if not all the other wheels were put in motion by this firft fpring. Now let us confider how far this was the cafe in fact.

To begin with the worft part of him,-----I faid he was a man of no fenfe of religion, or at leaft no other fenfe of it, but that which ferved his turn-----for he is recorded to have built temples in Judea, and erected images in them for idolatrous worfhip,-----not from a perfuafion of do-

ing

ing right, for he was bred a Jew, and confequently taught to abhor all idolatry,------but he was in truth facrificing all this time to a greater idol of his own, his ruling paffion ; for if we may truft Jofephus, his fole view in fo grofs a compliance was to ingratiate himfelf with Auguftus and the great men of Rome from whom he held his power.-----With this he was greedy and rapacious----how could he be otherwife with fo devouring an appetite as ambition to provide for ?------He was jealous in his nature, and fufpicious of all the world.---Shew me an ambitious man that is not fo; for as fuch a man's hand, like Ifhmael's, is againft every man, he concludes that every man's hand in courfe is againft his.

FEW men were ever guilty of more
aftonifhing

aftonifhing acts of cruelty------and yet the particular inftances of them in Herod were fuch as he was hurried into, by the alarms this waking paf-fion perpetually gave him.   He put the whole Sanhedrim to the fword ----fparing neither age, or wifdom, or merit----- one cannot fuppofe, fim-ply from an inclination to cruelty -----no----they had oppofed the efta-blifhment of his power at Jerufalem.

His own fons, two hopeful youths, he cut off by a public execution.-----The worft men have natural affec-tion-----and fuch a ftroke as this would run fo contrary to the natu-ral workings of it, that you are for-ced to fuppofe the impulfe of fome more violent inclination to over-rule and conquer it.-----And fo it was, for the Jewifh hiftorian tells us, 'twas

jealoufy

jealousy of power,---his darling object---of which he feared they would one day or other dispossess him------ sufficient inducement to transport a man of such a temper into the blackest excesses.

THUS far this one fatal and extravagant passion, accounts for the dark side of Herod's character. This governing principle being first laid open ------all his other bad actions follow in course, like so many symptomatic complaints from the same distemper.

LET us see, if this was not the case even of his virtues too.

AT first sight it seems a mystery--- how a man, so black as Herod has been thus far described------should be able to support himself, in the favour and

friendship

friendſhip of ſo wiſe and penetrating a body of men, as the Roman ſenate, of whom he held his power. To counter-balance the weight of ſo bad and deteſted a character---and be able to bear it up as Herod did, one would think he muſt have been maſter of ſome great ſecret worth enquiring after-----he was ſo. But that ſecret was no other than what appears on this reverſe of his character. He was a perſon of great addreſs----- popular in his outward behaviour.----- He was generous, prince-like in his entertainments and expences. The world was then as corrupt at leaſt, as now-----and Herod underſtood it ------knew at what price it was to be bought——and what qualities would bid the higheſt for its good word and approbation.

AND

AND in truth, he judged this matter fo well————that notwithftanding the general odium and prepof-
feffion which arofe againft fo hateful
a character-----in fpight of all the ill
impreffions, from fo many repeated
complaints of his cruelties and op-
preffions————he yet ftemmed the tor-
rent————and by the fpecious difplay
of thefe popular virtues bore himfelf
up againft it all his life.   So that at
length, when he was fummoned to
Rome to anfwer for his crimes------
Jofephus tells us———— that by the mere
magnificence of his expences-----and
the apparent generofity of his behaviour, he entirely confuted the whole
charge------and fo ingratiated himfelf
with the Roman fenate————and won
the heart of Auguftus——(as he had
that of Anthony before) that he ever
after had his favour and kindnefs;
                              which

which I cannot mention without adding------that it is an eternal ftain upon the character and memory of Auguftus, that he fold his countenance and protection to fo bad a man, for fo mean and bafe a confideration.

FROM this point of view, if we look back upon Herod---his beft qualities will fhrink into little room, and how glittering foever in appearance, when brought to this balance, are found wanting. And in truth, if we would not willingly be deceived in the value of any virtue or fet of virtues in fo complex a character— we muft call them to this very account; examine whom they ferve, what paffion and what principle they have for their mafter. When this is underftood, the whole is unravelled at once, and the character of Herod,

rod, as complicated as it is given in history------when thus analyfed, is fummed up in three words------*That he was a man of unbounded ambition, who ftuck at nothing to gratify it,*------ fo that not only his vices were miniſterial to his ruling paſſion, but his virtues too (if they deſerve the name) were drawn in, and liſted into the fame fervice.

Thus much for the character of Herod-----the critical review of which has many obvious ufes, to which I may truſt you, having time but to mention that particular one which firſt led me into this examination, namely, that all objections againſt the evangeliſt's account of this day's ſlaughter of the Bethlemitiſh infants —from the incredibility of fo horrid an account-----are filenced by this ac-

count of the man ; fince in this, he
acted but like himfelf, and juft fo
as you would expect in the fame
circumftances, from every man of
fo ambitious a head---and fo bad a
heart.------Confider, what havock
ambition has made—how often the
fame tragedy has been acted upon
larger theatres-----where not only the
innocence of childhood-----or the grey
hairs of the aged, have found no pro-
tection-----but whole countries without diftinction have been put to the
fword, or what is as cruel, have been
driven forth to nakednefs and famine to make way for new ones under the guidance of this paffion.-----
For a fpecimen of this, reflect upon
the ftory related by Plutarch :——
when by order of the Roman fenate,
feventy populous cities were una-
wares facked and deftroyed at one

prefixed

prefixed hour, by P. Æmilius—by whom one hundred and fifty thousand unhappy people were driven in one day into captivity—to be fold to the higheft bidder to end their days in cruel labour and anguifh. As aftonifhing as the account before us is, it vanifhes into nothing from fuch views, fince it is plain from all hiftory, that there is no wickednefs too great for fo unbounded a caufe, and that the moft horrid accounts in hiftory are, as I faid above, but too probable effects of it.————

MAY God of his mercy defend mankind from future experiments of this kind————and grant we may make a proper ufe of them, for the fake of Jefus Chrift, *Amen*.

SERMON X.

JOB's Account of the Shortness and Troubles of Life, confidered.

SERMON X.

JOB xiv. 1, 2.

Man that is born of a woman, is of few days, and full of trouble.-----He cometh forth like a flower, and is cut down; he fleeth also as a shadow, and continueth not.

THERE is something in this reflection of holy Job's, upon the shortness of life, and instability of human affairs, so beautiful and truly sublime; that one might challenge the writings of the most celebrated orators of antiquity, to produce a specimen of eloquence, so noble and thoroughly affecting. Whether this effect be owing in some measure, to the pathetic nature of the

subject

subject reflected on;---or to the east-
ern manner of expression, in a stile
more exalted and suitable to so great
a subject, or (which is the more likely account,) because they are properly the words of that Being, who first
inspired man with language, and
taught his mouth to utter, who o-
pened the lip of the dumb, and made
the tongue of the infant eloquent;
-- to which of these we are to refer
the beauty and sublimity of this, as
well as that of numberless other
passages in holy writ, may not seem
now material ; but surely without
these helps, never man was better
qualified to make just and noble
reflections upon the shortness of life,
and instability of human affairs, than
Job was, who had himself waded
through such a sea of troubles, and
in his passage had encountered many
vicissitudes

viciffitudes of ftorms and funfhine,
and by turns had felt both the
extremes, of all the happinefs, and
all the wretchednefs that mortal man
is heir to.

The beginning of his days was
crowned with every thing that ambition could wifh for,—he was the
greateft of all the men of the Eaft,
——had large and unbounded poffeffions, and no doubt enjoyed all
the comforts and advantages of life,
which they could adminifter.——Perhaps you will fay, a wife man might
not be inclined to give a full loofe
to this kind of happinefs, without
fome better fecurity for the fupport
of it, than the mere poffeffion of fuch
goods of fortune, which often flip
from under us, and fometimes
unaccountably make themfelves

wings, and fly away.—But he had that fecurity too,—for the hand of providence which had thus far protected, was ftill leading him forwards, and feemed engaged in the prefervation and continuance of thefe bleffings;——God had fet a hedge about him, and about all that he had on every fide, he had bleffed all the works of his hands, and his fubftance increafed every day. Indeed even with this fecurity, riches to him that hath *neither child or brother*, as the wife man obferves, inftead of a comfort prove fometimes a fore travel and vexation.—The mind of man is not always fatisfied with the reafonable affurance of its own enjoyments, but will look forwards, and if it difcovers fome imaginary void, the want of fome beloved object to fill his place after him, will often difquiet

quiet itſelf in vain, and ſay——" For whom do I labour, and bereave myſelf of reſt?"

THIS bar to his happineſs God had likewiſe taken away, in bleſſing him with a numerous offspring of ſons and daughters, the apparent inheriters of all his preſent happineſs.—— Pleaſing reflection! to think the bleſſings God has indulged one's ſelf in, ſhall be handed and continued down to a man's own ſeed; how little does this differ from a ſecond enjoyment of them, to an affectionate parent, who naturally looks forwards with as ſtrong an intereſt upon his children, as if he was to live over again in his own poſterity.

WHAT could be wanting to finiſh ſuch a picture of a happy man?——
C 6 Surely

Surely nothing, except a virtuous difpofition to give a relifh to thefe bleffings, and direct him to make a proper ufe of them.——He had that too, for he was a perfect and upright man, one that feared God and efchewed evil.

In the midft of all this profperity, which was as great as could well fall to the fhare of one man;---whilft all the world looked gay, and fmiled upon him, and every thing round him feemed to promife, if poffible, an increafe of happinefs, in one inftant all is changed into forrow and utter defpair.——

It pleafes God for wife purpofes to blaft the fortunes of his houfe, and cut off the hopes of his pofterity, and in one mournful day, to bring

this

this great prince from his palace down
to the dunghill. His flocks and herds,
in which confifted the abundance of
his wealth, were part confumed by a
fire from heaven, the remainder
taken away by the fword of the e-
nemy: his fons and daughters, whom
'tis natural to imagine fo good a man
had fo brought up in a fenfe of their
duty, as to give him all reafonable
hopes of much joy and pleafure in
their future lives;——natural profpect for a parent to look towards at,
to recompenfe him for the many
cares and anxieties which their in-
fancy had coft him! thefe dear pled-
ges of his future happinefs were all,
all fnatched from him at one blow,
juft at the time that one might imagine they were beginning to be the
comfort and delight of his old age,
which moft wanted fuch ftaves to
lean

lean on ;---and as circumſtances add to an evil, ſo they did to this;—— for it fell out not only by a very calamitous accident, which was grievous enough in itſelf, but likewiſe upon the back of his other misfortunes, when he was ill prepared to bear ſuch a ſhock; and what would ſtill add to it, it happened at an hour when he had leaſt reaſon to expect it, when he would naturally think his children ſecure and out of the way of danger. "For whilſt they were feaſting and making merry in their eldeſt brother's houſe, a great wind out of the wilderneſs ſmote the four corners of the houſe, and it fell upon them."

Such a concurrence of misfortunes are not the common lot of many: and yet there are inſtances of ſome
who

who have undergone as severe trials, and bravely struggled under them; perhaps by natural force of spirits, the advantages of health, and ·the cordial assistance of a friend. And with these helps, what may not a man sustain?---But this was not Job's case, for scarce had these evils fallen upon him, when he was not only borne down with a grievous distemper which afflicted him from the crown of his head to the sole of his foot, but likewise his three friends, in whose kind consolations he might have found a medicine,---even the wife of his bosom, whose duty it was with a gentle hand to have softened all his sorrows, instead of doing this, they cruelly insulted and became the reproachers of his integrity. O God! what is man when thou thus bruisest him, and makest his burthen hea-

vier

vier as his ftrength grows lefs?———
Who, that had found himfelf thus
an example of the many changes and
chances of this mortal life;——when
he confidered himfelf now ftripped
and left deftitute of fo many valua-
ble bleffings which the moment before thy providence had poured upon his head,—when he reflected upon this gay delightfome ftructure, in
appearance fo ftrongly built, fo plea-
fingly furrounded with every thing
that could flatter his hopes and
wifhes, and beheld it all levelled with
the ground in one moment, and the
whole piofpect vanifh with it like the
defcription of an enchantment;—
who I fay that had feen and felt the
fhock of fo fudden a revolution,
would not have been furnifhed with
juft and beautiful reflections upon
the occafion, and faid with Job in
the

the words of the text, " That man that is born of a woman, is of few days, and full of mifery,——that he cometh forth like a flower, and is cut down; he fleeth alfo as a fhadow, and continueth not."

THE words of the text are an e-pitome of the *natural* and *moral* va-nity of man, and contain two di-ftinct declarations concerning his ftate and condition in each refpect.

FIRST, that he is a creature of few days; and, fecondly, that thofe days are full of trouble.

I SHALL make fome reflections up-on each of thefe in their order, and conclude with a practical leffon from the whole.

AND

AND, firſt, that he is of few days. The compariſon which Job makes uſe of, That man cometh forth like a flower, is extremely beautiful, and more to the purpoſe than the moſt elaborate pıoof, which in truth the ſubjeƈt will not eaſily admit of;---the ſhortneſs of life being a point ſo generally complained of in all ages ſince the flood, and ſo univerſally felt and acknowledged by the whole ſpecies, as to require no evidence beyond a ſimilitude; the intent of which is not ſo much to prove the faƈt, as to illuſtrate and place it in ſuch a light as to ſtrike us, and bring the impreſſion home to ourſelves in a more affeƈting manner.

MAN comes forth, ſays Job, like a flower, and is cut down;——he is ſent into the world the faireſt and

nobleſt.

noblest part of God's works,——fa-
shioned after the image of his Crea-
tor with respect to reason and the
great faculties of the mind; he cometh forth glorious as the flower of
the field ; as it surpasses the vegetable world in beauty, so does he the
animal world in the glory and excel-
lencies of his nature.

The one——if no untimely accident oppress it, soon arrives at the
full period of its perfection,——is suf-
fered to triumph for a few moments,
and is plucked up by the roots in
the very pride and gayest stage of
its being :——or if it happens to escape
the hands of violence, in a few days
it necessarily sickens of itself and
dies away.

Man, likewise, though his pro-
gress

grefs is flower, and his duration fomething longer, yet the periods of his growth and declenfion are nearly the fame both in the nature and manner of them.

IF he efcapes the dangers which threaten his tenderer years, he is foon got into the full maturity and ftrength of life, and if he is fo fortunate as not to be hurried out of it then by accidents, by his own folly and intemperance——if he efcapes thefe, he naturally decays of himfelf; ——a period comes faft upon him, beyond which he was not made to laft.——Like a flower or fruit which may be plucked up by force before the time of their maturity, yet cannot be made to outgrow the period when they are to fade and drop of themfelves; when that comes, the

hand.

hand of nature then plucks them both off, and no art of the botanift can uphold the one, or fkill of the phyfician preferve the other, beyond the periods to which their original frames and conftitutions were made to extend. As God has appointed and determined the feveral growths and decays of the vegetable race, fo he feems as evidently to have prefcribed the fame laws to man, as well as all living creatures, in the firft rudiments of which, there are contained the fpecifick powers of their growth, duration and extinction; and when the evolutions of thofe a-nimal powers are exhaufted and run down, the creature expires and dies of itfelf, as ripe fruit falls from the tree, or a flower preferved beyond its bloom drops and perifhes upon the ftalk.

THUS

THUS much for this comparison of Job's, which though it is very poetical, yet conveys a juft idea of the thing referred to.------" That he fleeth alfo as a fhadow, and continueth not"—is no lefs a faithful and fine reprefentation of the fhortnefs and vanity of human life, of which one cannot give a better explanation, than by referring to the original, from whence the picture was taken.—— With how quick a fucceffion, do days, months, and years, pafs over our heads?—how truly like a fhadow that departeth do they flee away infenfibly, and fcarce leave an impreffion with us?——when we endeavour to call them back by reflection, and confider in what manner they have gone, how unable are the beft of us to give a tolerable account?—and were it not for fome of the more remarkable

markable ſtages which have diſtin-
guiſhed a few periods of this rapid
piogreſs——we ſhould look back upon it all as Nebuchadnezzar did upon his dream when he awoke in the
morning,——he was ſenſible many
things had paſſed, and troubled him
too; but had paſſed on ſo quickly,
they had left no footſteps behind, by
which he could be enabled to trace
them back.---Melancholy account of
the life of man! which generally runs
on in ſuch a manner, as ſcarce to al-
low time to make reflections which
way it has gone.

How many of our firſt years ſlide
by, in the innocent ſports of childhood, in which we are not able to
make reflections upon them?——how
many more thoughtleſs years eſcape
us in our youth, when we are unwilling

THUS much for this comparison of Job's, which though it is very poetical, yet conveys a juſt idea of the thing referred to.------" That he fleeth alſo as a ſhadow, and continueth not"—is no leſs a faithful and fine repreſentation of the ſhortneſs and vanity of human life, of which one cannot give a better explanation, than by referring to the original, from whence the picture was taken.—— With how quick a ſucceſſion, do days, months, and years, paſs over our heads ?—how truly like a ſhadow that departeth do they flee away inſenſibly, and ſcarce leave an impreſſion with us ?——when we endeavour to call them back by reflection, and conſider in what manner they have gone, how unable are the beſt of us to give a tolerable account ?—and were it not for ſome of the more remarkable

markable ſtages which have diſtin-
guiſhed a few periods of this rapid
progreſs——we ſhould look back upon it all as Nebuchadnezzar did upon his dream when he awoke in the
morning ;——he was ſenſible many
things had paſſed, and troubled him
too; but had paſſed on ſo quickly,
they had left no footſteps behind, by
which he could be enabled to trace
them back.---Melancholy account of
the life of man ! which generally runs
on in ſuch a manner, as ſcarce to al-
low time to make reflections which
way it has gone.

How many of our firſt years ſlide
by, in the innocent ſports of childhood, in which we are not able to
make reflections upon them ?——how
many more thoughtleſs years eſcape
us in our youth, when we are unwilling

willing to do it, and are fo eager in the purfuit of pleafure as to have no time to fpare, to ftop and confider them ?

WHEN graver and riper years come on, and we begin to think it time to reform and fet up for men of fenfe and conduct, then the bufinefs and perplexing interefts of this world, and the endlefs plotting and contriving how to make the moft of it, do fo wholly employ us, that we are too bufy to make reflections upon fo unprofitable a fubject.——As families and children increafe, fo do our affections, and with them are multiplied our cares and toils for their prefervation and eftablifhment ;——all which take up our thoughts fo clofely, and poffefs them fo long, that we are often overtaken by grey hairs before

fore we fee them, or have found leifure to confider how far we were
got,—what we have been doing,—
and for what puipofe God fent us
into the world. As man may juftly
be faid to be of few days confidered
with refpect to this hafty fucceffion
of things, which foon carries him into the decline of his life, fo may he
likewife be faid to flee like a fhadow
and continue not, when his duration is compared with other parts of
God's works, and even the works
of his own hands, which outlaft him
many generations ;—whilft his—as
Homer obferves, like leaves, one ge-
neration drops, and another fprings
up to fall again and be forgotten.

BUT when we further confider his
days in the light in which we ought
chiefly to view them, as they appear

in thy fight, O GOD! with whom a
thoufand years are but as yefterday;
when we reflect that this hand-breadth
of life is all that is meafured out to
us from that eternity for which he is
created, how does his fhort fpan vanifh to nothing in the comparifon?
'Tis true, the greateft portion of time
will do the fame when compared with
what is to come; and therefore fo
fhort and tranfitory a one, as three-
fcore years and ten, beyond which
all is declared to be labour and forrow, may the eafier be allowed: and
yet how uncertain are we of that
portion, fhort as it is? Do not ten
thoufand accidents break off the
flender thread of human life, long
before it can be drawn out to that
extent?—The new-born babe falls
down an eafy prey, and moulders
back again into duft, like a tender

bloffom

bloſſom put forth in an untimely hour.——The hopeful youth in the very pride and beauty of life is cut off, ſome cruel diſtemper or unthought of accident lays him proſtrate upon the earth, to purſue Job's compaiiſon, like a blooming flower ſmit and ſhuivelled up with a malignant blaſt. ——In this ſtage of life chances multiply upon us,——the ſeeds of diſorders are ſown by intemperance or neglect,——infectious diſtempers are more eaſily contracted, when contracted they rage with greater violence, and the ſuccefs in many caſes is more doubtful, infomuch that they who have exerciſed themſelves in computations of this kind tell us, " That one half of the whole ſpecies which are born into the world, go out of it again, and are all dead

in fo fhort a fpace as the firft feven-
teen years.

THESE reflections may be fufficient
to illuftrate the firft part of Job's declaration, " *That man is of few days.*"
Let us examine the truth of the o-
ther, and fee, whether he is not likewife full of trouble.

AND here we muft not take our
account from the flattering outfide
of things, which are generally fet
off with a glittering appearance e-
nough, efpecially in what is called,
higher life.——Nor can we fafely truft
the evidence of fome of the more
merry and thoughtlefs amongft us,
who are fo fet upon the enjoyment
of life as feldom to reflect upon the
troubles of it ;—or who, perhaps, becaufe they are not yet come to this

portion

portion of their inheritance, imagine
it is not their common lot.——Nor,
laftly, are we to form an idea of it,
from the delufive ftories of a few of
the moft profperous paffengers, who
have fortunately failed through and
efcaped the rougher toils and diftref-
fes. But we are to take our account
from a clofe furvey of human life,
and the real face of things, ftript of
every thing that can palliate or gild
it over. We muft hear the general
complaint of all ages, and read the
hiftories of mankind. If we look
into them, and examine them to the
bottom, what do they contain but
the hiftory of fad and uncomfortable
paffages, which a good-natured man
cannot read but with oppreffion of
fpirits.——Confider the dreadful
fucceffion of wars in one part or o-
ther of the earth, perpetuated from

one century to another with so little in-
termission, that mankind have scarce
had time to breathe from them, since
ambition first came into the world;
consider the horrid effects of them
in all those barbarous devastations
we read of, where whole nations have
been put to the sword, or have been
driven out to nakedness and famine
to make room for new comers.——
Consider how great a part of our species in all ages down to this, have
been trod under the feet of cruel and
capricious tyrants, who would neither hear their cries, nor pity their
distresses.———Consider slavery,——
what it is,---how bitter a draught,
and how many millions have been
made to drink of it ;---which if it can
poison all earthly happiness when exercised barely upon our bodies, what
must it be, when it comprehends
both

both the flavery of body and mind?
———To conceive this, look into the
hiftory of the Romifh church and her
tyrants, (or rather executioners) who
feem to have taken pleafure in the
pangs and convulfions of their fellow-creatures.———Examine the in-
quifition, hear the melancholy notes
founded in every cell.———Confider
the anguifh of mock-trials, and the
exquifite tortures confequent thereupon, mercilefsly inflicted upon the
unfortunate, where the racked and
weary foul has fo often wifhed to take
its leave,—but cruelly not fuffered
to depart.———Confider how many of
thefe helplefs wretches have been ha-
led from thence in all periods of this
tyrannic ufurpation, to undergo the
maffacres and flames to which a falfe
and a bloody religion has condemned them.

If

IF this sad history and detail of the more public causes of the miseries of man are not sufficient, let us behold him in another light with respect to the more private causes of them, and see whether he is not full of trouble likewise there, and almost born to it as naturally as the sparks fly upwards. If we consider man as a creature full of wants and necessities (whether real or imaginary) which he is not able to supply of himself, what a train of disappointments, vexations and dependencies are to be seen, issuing from thence to perplex and make his being uneasy?——How many just-lings and hard struggles do we undergo in making our way in the world?— How barbarously held back? ——How often and basely over-thrown, in aiming only at getting bread?——How many of us never at-

tain

tak it—at leaſt not comfortably,—
but from various unknown cauſes---
eat it all their lives long in bitterneſs?

IF we ſhift the ſcene, and look
upwards, towards thoſe whoſe ſituation in life ſeems to place them above
the ſorrows of this kind, yet where
are they exempt from others? Do
not all ranks and conditions of men
meet with ſad accidents and num-
berleſs calamities in other reſpects,
which often make them go heavily
all their lives long?

How many fall into chronical infirmities, which render both their
days and nights reſtleſs and inſup-
portable?---How many of the higheſt
rank are tore up with ambition, or
ſoured with diſappointments, and

how many more from a thoufand fecret caufes of difquiet 'pine away in
filence, and owe their deaths to forrow and dejection of heart?——If we
caft our eyes upon the loweft clafs
and condition of life,—— the fcene is
more melancholy ftill.——Millions
of our fellow-creatures, born to no
inheritance but poverty and trouble,
forced by the neceffity of their lots
to drudgery and painful employ-
ments, and hard fet with that too,
to get enough to keep themfelves
and families alive.——So that upon
the whole, when we have examined
the true ftate and condition of human life, and have made fome al-
lowances for a few fugacious, deceitful pleafures, there is fcarce any
thing to be found which contradicts
Job's defcription of it.——Which e-
ver

ver way we look abroad, we fee fome legible characters of what God firft denounced againft us, " That in forrow we fhould eat our bread, till we return to the ground, from whence we were taken *."

But fome one will fay, Why are we thus to be put out of love with human life? To what purpofe is it to expofe the dark fides of it to us, or enlarge upon the infirmities which are natural, and confequently out of our power to redrefs?

I ANSWER, that the fubject is neverthelefs of great importance, fince it is neceffary every creature fhould underftand his prefent ftate and con-

D 6   dition,

---

* N.B Moft of thefe reflections upon the miferies of life are taken from Woollafton.

dition, to put him in mind of behaving fuitably to it.———Does not an impartial furvey of man———the holding up this glafs to fhew him his defects and natural infirmities, naturally tend to cure his pride and cloath him with humility, which is a drefs that beft becomes a fhort-lived and a wretched creature?—Does not the confideration of the fhortnefs of our life, convince us of the wifdom of dedicating fo fmall a portion to the great purpofes of eternity?

LASTLY, When we reflect that this fpan of life, fhort as it is, is chequered with fo many troubles, that there is nothing in this world fprings up, or can be enjoyed without a mixture of forrow, how infenfibly does it incline us to turn our

eyes

eyes and affections from fo gloomy a profpect, and fix them upon that happier country, where afflictions cannot follow us, and where God will wipe away all tears from off our faces for ever and ever? Amen.

SER-

SERMON XI.

EVIL-SPEAKING.

SERMON XI.

JAMES i. 26.

If any man among you seem to be religious, and bridleth not his tongue, but deceiveth his own heart, that man's religion is vain.

OF the many duties owing both to God and our neighbour, there are scarce any men so bad, as not to acquit themselves of some, and few so good, I fear, as to practise all.

EVERY man seems willing enough to compound the matter, and adopt so much of the system, as will at least interfere with his principal and ruling passion, and for those parts,
which

which would occasion a more trou-
blesome opposition, to consider them
as hard sayings, and so leave them
for those to practise, whose natural
tempers are better suited for the
struggle. So that a man shall be covetous, oppressive, revengeful, neither a lover of truth, or common
honesty, and yet at the same time,
shall be *very* religious, and so sancti-
fied, as not once to fail of paying
his morning and evening sacrifice to
God. So, on the other hand, a man
shall live without God in the world,
have neither any great sense of religion, or indeed pretend to have any,
and yet be of nicest honour, consci-
entiously just and fair in all his dealings. And here it is that men generally betray themselves, deceiving,
as the apostle says, their own hearts;
of which the instances are so various,

ous, in one degree or other throughout human life, that one might safely say, the bulk of mankind live in such a contradiction to themselves, that there is no character so hard to be met with as one, which upon a critical examination will appear altogether uniform, and in every point consistent with itself.

If such a contrast was only observable in the different stages of a man's life, it would cease to be either a matter of wonder, or of just reproach. Age, experience, and much reflection, may naturally enough be supposed to alter a man's sense of things, and so entirely to transform him, that not only in outward appearances, but in the very cast and turn of his mind, he may be as unlike and different from the

man

man he was twenty or thirty years
ago, as he ever was from any thing
of his own species.   This, I say, is
naturally to be accounted for, and
in some cases might be praise-worthy
too ; but the observation is to be
made of men in the same period of
their lives, that in the same day,
sometimes in the very same action,
they are utterly inconsistent and ir-
reconcileable with themselves.---Look
at a man in one light, and he shall
seem wise, penetrating, discreet, and
brave : behold him in another point
of view, and you see a creature all
over folly and indiscretion, weak and
timorous, as cowardice and indiscretion can make him.   A man shall
appear gentle, courteous, and benevolent to all mankind ; follow him
into his own house, may be you see
a tyrant, morose and savage to all,
whose

whose happiness depends upon his kindness. A third in his general behaviour is found to be generous, disinterested, humane and friendly,---hear but the sad story of the friendless orphans, too creduloully trusting all their little substance into his hands, and he shall appear more sordid, more pitiless and unjust, than the injured themselves have bitterness to paint him. Another shall be charitable to the poor, uncharitable in his censures and opinions of all the rest of the world beside;——temperate in his appetites, intemperate in his tongue; shall have too much conscience and religion to cheat the man who trusts him, and perhaps as far as the business of debtor and creditor extends, shall be just and scrupulous to the uttermost mite ; yet in matters of full as great concern, where he is to

have

have the handling of the parties reputation and good name,—the dear-
est, the tenderest property the man
has, he will do him irreparable da-
mage, and rob him there without
measure or pity.---

And this seems to be that particular piece of inconsistency and contradiction which the text is levelled
at, in which the words seem so pointed, as if St. James had known more
flagrant instances of this kind of de-
lusion than what had fallen under
the observation of any of the rest of
the apostles; he being more remark-
ably vehement and copious upon that
subject than any other.

Doubtless some of his converts
had been notoriously wicked and li-
centious, in this remorseless practice
of

of defamation and evil-fpeaking. Perhaps the holy man, though fpot-lefs as an angel, (for no character is too facred for calumny to blacken), had grievoufly fuffered himfelf, and as his bleffed Mafter foretold him, had been cruelly reviled, and evil *fpoken* of.

ALL his labours in the gofpel, his unaffected and perpetual folicitude for the prefervation of his flock, his watchings, his faftings, his poverty, his natural fimplicity and innocence of life, *all* perhaps were not enough to defend him from this unruly wea-pon, fo full of deadly poifon. And what in all likelihood might move his forrow and indignation more, fome who feemed the moft devout and zealous of all his converts, were the moft mercilefs and uncharitable

in

in that refpect. Having a form of godlinefs, full of bitter envying and ftrife.

WITH fuch it is that he expoftulates fo largely in the third chapter of his epiftle; and there is fomething in his vivacity tempered with fuch affection and concern, as well fuited the character of an infpired man. My brethren, fays the apoftle, thefe things ought not to be.------The wifdom that is from above is pure, peaceable, gentle, full of mercy, without partiality, without hypocrify. The wifdom from above, ---that heavenly religion which I have preached to you, is pure, alike and confiftent with itfelf in all its parts; like its great Author, 'tis univerfally kind and benevolent in all cafes and circumftances. Its firft glad tidings,

were

were peace upon earth, good-will towards men; its chief corner-ftone, its moft diftinguifhing character is love, that kind principle which brought it down, in the pure exercife of which confifts the chief enjoyment of heaven from whence it came. But this practice, my brethren, cometh not from above, but is earthly, fenfual, devilifh, full of confufion and every evil work. Reflect then a moment; can a fountain fend forth at the fame place, fweet water and bitter? Can the fig-tree, my brethren, bear olive-berries, either a vine, figs? Lay your hands upon your hearts, and let your confciences fpeak.---Ought not the fame juft principle which reftrains you from cruelty and wrong in one cafe, equally to with-hold you from it in another?---Should not charity and good will like the principle of life, circulating through the fmalleft veffels in every member, ought it not to operate as regularly upon you, throughout, as well upon your words, as upon your actions?

If a man is wife and endued with knowledge, let him fhew it, out of a good converfation, with meeknefs of wifdom. But---if any man a-mongft you, feemeth to be religious ---feemeth to be,------for truly religious he cannot be,------and bridleth not his tongue, but deceiveth his own heart, this man's religion is vain.------- This is the full force of St. James's reafoning, upon which I have dwelt the more, it being the foundation, upon which is grounded this clear decifion of the matter left us in the text. In which the apoftle feems to

have

have set the two characters of a saint and a slanderer at such a variance, that one would have thought they could never have had a heart to have met together again. But there are no alliances too strange for this world. ——How many may we observe every day, even of the gentler sex, as well as our own, who without conviction of doing much wrong, in the midst of a full career of calumny and defamation, rise up punctual at the stated hour of prayer, leave the cruel story half untold till they return,---go,---and kneel down before the throne of heaven, thank God that he had not made them like others, and that his Holy Spirit had enabled them to perform the duties of the day, in so Christian and conscientious a manner!

THIS

THIS delufive itch for flander, too common in all ranks of people, whether to gratify a little ungenerous refentment;——whether oftener out of a principle of levelling from a narrowneſs and poverty of foul, ever impatient of merit and fuperiority in others; whether a mean ambition or the infatiate luſt of being witty, (a talent in which ill-nature and malice are no ingredients,)——or laſtly, whether from a natural cruelty of difpofition, abftraċted from all views and confiderations of felf: to which one, or whether to all jointly we are indebted for this contagious malady; thus much is certain, from whatever feeds it fprings, the growth and progreſs of it are as deftructive to, as they are unbecoming a civilized people. To paſs a hard and ill-natured reflection, upon an unde-

.

figning

figning action; to invent, or which is equally bad, to propagate a vexatious report, without colour and grounds; to plunder an innocent man of his character and good name, a jewel which perhaps he has ftarved himfelf to purchafe, and probably would hazard his life to fecure; to rob him at the fame time of his happinefs and peace of mind; perhaps his bread,————the bread may be of a virtuous family; and all this, as Solomon fays of the madman, who cafteth fire-brands, arrows, and death, and faith, Am I not in fport? all this, out of wantonnefs, and oftener fiom worfe motives; the whole appears fuch a complication of badnefs, as requires no words or warmth of fancy to aggravate. Pride, treachery, envy, hypocrify, malice, cruelty, and felf-love, may have been faid in

E 3   one

one fhape or other, to have occafion-
ed all the frauds and mifchiefs that
ever happened in the world ; but the
chances againft a coincidence of them
all in one perfon are fo many, that
one would have fuppofed the character of a common flanderer as rare
and difficult a production in nature,
as that of a great genius, which feldom happens above once in an age.

BUT whatever was the cafe, when
St. James wrote his epiftle, we have
been very fuccefsful in later days,
and have found out the art, by a
proper management of light and
fhade, to compound all thefe vices
together, fo as to give body and
ftrength to the whole, whilft no one
but a difcerning artift is able to difcover the labours that join in finifh-
ing the picture.—And indeed, like
many

many other bad originals in the
world,---it ftands in need of all the
difguife it has.——For who could be
enamoured of a character, made up
of fo loathfome a compound,——could
they behold it naked,——in its crooked
and deformed fhape,———with all its
natural and detefted infirmities laid
open to public view ?

AND therefore, it were to be wifhed, that one could do in this malignant cafe of the mind,———what is generally done for the public good, in
the more malignant and epidemical
cafes of the body,-----that is,——— when
they are found infectious,———to
write a hiftory of the diftemper,-----
and afcertain all the fymptoms of the
malady, fo that every one might
know, whom he might venture to
go near, with tolerable fafety to him-

E 4 felf.

felf.—But alas! the fymptoms of this appear in fo many ftrange, and contradictory fhapes, and vary fo wonderfully with the temper and habit of the patient, that they are not to be claffed,——or reduced to one regular fyftem.

TEN thoufand are the vehicles, in which this deadly poifon is prepared and communicated to the world,------ and by fome artful hands, 'tis done by fo fubtle and nice an infufion, that it is not to be tafted or difcovered, but by its effects.

How frequently is the honefty and integrity of a man, difpofed of, by a fmile or a fhrug?—How many good and generous actions, have been funk into oblivion, by a diftruftful look, ---or ftampt with the imputation of

proceeding

proceeding from bad motives, by a mysterious and seasonable whisper?

Look into companies of those whose gentle natures should disarm them,——we shall find no better account.——How large a portion of chastity is sent out of the world by distant hints,——nodded away, and cruelly winked into suspicion, by the envy of those who are past all temptation of it themselves.---How often does the reputation of a helpless creature bleed by a report——which the party, who is at the pains to propagate it, beholds with much pity and fellow-feeling,—that she is heartily sorry for it,—hopes in God it is not true;---however, as Archbishop Tillotson wittily observes upon it, is resolved in the mean time to give the report her pass, that at least

E 5

it

it may have fair play to take its fortune in the world,—to be believed
or not, according to the charity of
thofe, into whofe hands it fhall hap-
pen to fall.

So fruitful is this vice in variety
of expedients, to fatiate as well as
difguife itfelf. But if thefe fmooth-
er weapons cut fo fore,———what
fhall we fay of open and unblufhing
fcandal---fubjected to no caution,---
tied down to no reftraints?---If the
one, like an arrow fhot in the dark,
does neverthelefs fo much fecret mifchief,------this like the peftilence,
which rageth at noon-day, fweeps
all before it, levelling without diftinction the good and the bad; a
thoufand fall befide it, and ten thoufand on its right hand,———they fall,
-----fo rent and torn in this tender

part of them, fo unmercifully but-
chered, as fometimes never to reco-
ver either the wounds,---or the anguifh of heart,---which they have oc-
cafioned.---

But there is nothing fo bad which
will not admit of fomething to be
faid in its defence.

And here it may be afked,---Whe-
ther the inconveniencies and ill effects which the world feels,---from
the licentioufnefs of this practice----
are not fufficiently counterballanced
by the real influence it has upon
men's lives and conduct?---That if
there was no evil fpeaking in the
world, thoufands would be encou-
raged to do ill,---and would rufh into many indecorums, like a horfe in-

to

to the battle,---were they fure to e-
fcape the tongues of men.

THAT if we take a general view
of the world,———we fhall find that a
great deal of virtue,———at leaft of
the outward appearance of it,------is
not fo much from any fixed principle, as the terror of what the world
will fay,- ---and the liberty it will
take upon the occafions we fhall give.

THAT if we defcend to particulars,
numbers are every day taking more
pains to be well fpoken of,---than
what would actually enable them to
live fo as to deferve it.

THAT there are many of both fexes,
who can fupport life well enough,
without honour or chaftity,———who
without reputation, (which is but
the

the opinion which the world has of
the matter,) would hide their heads
in fhame, and fink down in utter
defpair of happinefs.---No doubt the
tongue is a weapon, which does cha-
ftife many indecorums, which the
laws of men will not reach,---and
keeps many in awe,---whom confcience will not,---and where the cafe
is indifputably flagrant,---the fpeaking of it in fuch words as it deferves,
---fcarce comes within the prohibi-
tion.---In many cafes, 'tis haid to exprefs ourfelves fo as to fix a diftinction betwixt oppofite characters,-----
and fometimes it may be as much a
debt we owe to virtue, and as great
a piece of juftice to expofe a vicious
character, and paint it in its proper
colours,------as it is to fpeak well of
the deferving, and defcribe his particular virtues.-------And, indeed,
when

when we inflict this punishment upon the bad, merely out of principle,
and without indulgences to any private paffion of our own,---'tis a cafe
which happens fo feldom, that one
might venture to except it.

However, to thofe, who in this
objection are really concerned for the
caufe of virtue, I cannot help re-
commending what would much more
effectually ferve her intereft, and be
a furer token of their zeal and attach-
ment to her. And that is,---in all
fuch plain inftances where it feems
to be duty, to fix a diftinction betwixt the good and the bad,---to let
their actions fpeak it, inftead of their
words, or at leaft to let them both
fpeak one language. We all of us
talk fo loud againft vicious characters, and are fo unanimous in our

cry

cry againſt them,---that an unexpe-
rienced man, who only truſted his
ears, would imagine the whole world
was in an uproar about it, and that
mankind were all aſſociating together,
to hunt vice utterly out of the world.
————Shift the ſcene,—and let him
behold the reception which vice meets
with,---he will ſee the conduct and behaviour of the world towards it, ſo
oppoſite to their declarations,—he
will find all he heard, ſo contradict-
ed by what he ſaw,---as to leave him
in doubt, which of his ſenſes he is
to truſt,---or in which of the two caſes, mankind were really in earneſt.
Was there virtue enough in the world
to make a general ſtand againſt this
contradiction,---that is,---was every
one who deſerved to be ill ſpoken of
---ſure to be ill looked on---too, was
it a certain conſequence of the loſs
of

of a man's character,---to lose his friends,---to lose the advantages of his birth and fortune,---and thenceforth be univerfally fhunned, univerfally flighted.——

WAS no quality a fhelter againft the indecorums of the other fex, but was every woman without diftinction,——who had juftly forfeited her reputation,---from that moment was fhe fure to forfeit likewife all claim to civility and refpect.——

OR, in a word,---could it be eftablifhed as a law in our ceremonial, ——that where-ever characters in either fex were become notorious,---it fhould be deemed infamous, either to pay or receive a vifit from them, and that the door be fhut againft them in all public places, till they had fa-

tisfied

tisfied the world, by giving testimony of a better life.----A few such plain and honest maxims faithfully put in practice,------would force us upon some degree of reformation. Till this is done,---it avails little that we have no mercy upon them with our tongues, since they escape without feeling any other inconvenience.

WE all cry out that the world is corrupt,------and I fear too justly;--- but we never reflect, what we have to thank for it, and that it is our open countenance of vice, which gives the lie to our private censures of it, which is its chief protection and encouragement.---To those however, who still believe, that evil-speaking is some terror to evil doers, one may answer, as a great man has done upon the occasion,---that after all our

exhortations

exhortations againſt it,---'tis not to be feared, but that there will be e-vil-ſpeaking enough left in the world to chaſtiſe the guilty,---and we may ſafely truſt them to an ill-natured world, that there will be no failure of juſtice upon this ſcore.------The paſſions of men are pretty ſevere ex-ecutioners, and to them let us leave this ungrateful taſk,------and rather ourſelves endeavour to cultivate that more friendly one, recommended by the apoſtle,---of letting all bitterneſs, and wrath, and clamour, and evil-ſpeaking, be put away from us,---of being kind to one another,---tender-hearted, forgiving one another, e-ven as God for Chriſt's ſake forgave us.   Amen.

SERMON XII.

JOSEPH's History
CONSIDERED.

Forgiveneſs of INJURIES.

SERMON XII.

GENESIS i. 15.

And when Joseph's brethren saw that their father was dead, they said, Joseph will peradventure hate us, and will certainly requite us all the evil which we did unto him.

THERE are few inftances of the exercife of particular virtues which feem harder to attain to, or which appear more amiable and engaging in themfelves, than thofe of moderation and the forgivenefs of injuries; and when the temptations againft them, happen to be heightened by the bitternefs of a provocation on one hand, and the fairnefs of an opportunity to retaliate on the other,

other, the inftances *then* are truly great and heroic. The words of the text, which are the confultation of the fons of Jacob amongft themfelves upon their father Ifrael's death, when becaufe it was in Jofeph's power to revenge the deadly injury they had formeily done him, they concluded in courfe, that it was in his intention, will lead us to a beautiful example of this kind in the character and behaviour of Jofeph confequent thereupon ; and as it feems a perfect and very engaging pattern of forbearance, it may not be improper to make it ferve for the ground-work of a difcourfe upon that fubject.—— The whole tranfaction from the firft occafion given by Jofeph in his youth, to this laft act of remiffion, at the conclufion of his life, may be faid to be a mafter-piece of hiftory. There

is

is not only in the manner throughout such a happy though uncommon
mixture of simplicity and grandeur,
which is a double character so hard
to be united, that it is seldom to be
met with in compositions merely human;------but it is likewise related
with the greatest variety of tender
and affecting circumstances, which
would afford matter for reflections
useful for the conduct of almost every part and stage of a man's life.-----
But as the words of the text, as well
as the intention and compass of this
discourse, particularly confine me to
speak only to one point, namely, the
forgiveness of injuries, it will be proper only to consider such circumstances of the story, as will place this
instance of it in its just light; and
then proceed to make a more general use of the great example of moderation

-deration and forbearance, which it
-fets before us.

It feems ftrange at firft fight, that
after the fons of Jacob had fallen into Jofeph's power, when they were
forced by the forenefs of the famine
to go down into Egypt to buy corn,
and had found him too good a man
even to expoftulate with them for
an injury, which he feemed then to
have digefted, and pioufly to have
refolved into the over-ruling providence of God, for the prefervation
of much people, how they could e-
ver after queftion the uprightnefs of
his intentions, or entertain the leaft
fufpicion that his reconciliation was
diffembled. Would not one have i-
magined, that the man who had difcovered fuch a goodnefs of foul, that
he fought where to weep, becaufe
he

he could not bear the ſtruggles of a counterfeited harſhneſs, could never be ſuſpected afterwards of intending a real one;---and that he only waited till their father Iſrael's death, to re-quite them all the evil which they had done unto him. What ſtill adds to this difficulty, is, that his affec-tionate manner in making himſelf known to them;-----his goodneſs in forbearing, not only to reproach them for the injury they had for-merly done him, but extenuating and excuſing the fault to themſelves, his comforting and ſpeaking kindly to them, and ſeconding all with the tendereſt marks of an undiſguiſed forgiveneſs, in falling upon their necks, and weeping aloud, that all the houſe of Pharaoh heard him;-----that moreover this behaviour of Jo-ſeph could not appear to them, to be the effect of any warm and fudden transport, which might as fuddenly give way to other reflections, but that it evidently fprung from a fettled principle of uncommon generofity in his nature, which was above the temptation of making ufe of an opportunity for revenge, which the courfe of God's providence had put into his hands for better purpofes; and what might ftill feem to confirm this, was the evidence of his actions to them afterwards, in bringing them and all their houfehold up out of Canaan, and placing them near him in the land of Gofhen, the richeft part of Egypt, where they had had fo many years experience of his love and kindnefs. And yet it is plain all this did not clear his motive from fufpicion, or at leaft themfelves of fome apprehenfions of a change in

his

his conduct towards them. And was
it not that the whole tranfaction was
wrote under the direction of the Spirit of truth, and that other hiftori-
ans concur in doing juftice to Jofeph's character, and fpeak of him
as a compaffionate, and merciful man,
one would be apt, you will fay, to
imagine here, that Mofes might poffibly have omitted fome circumftances of Jofeph's behaviour, which had
alarmed his brethren, betwixt the
time of his firft reconciliation and
that of their father's death.——For
they could not be fufpicious of his
intentions without fome caufe, and
fear where no fear was.---But does
not a guilty confcience often do fo?
and though it has the grounds, yet
wants the power to think itfelf fafe.

AND could we look into the hearts

F 2 of

of thofe who know they deferve ill, we fhould find many an inftance, where a kindnefs from an injured hand, where there was leaft reafon to expect one, has ftruck deeper and touched the heart with a degree of remorfe and concern, which perhaps no feverity or refentment could have reached. This reflection will in fome meafure help to explain this difficulty, which occurs in the ftory. For it is obfervable, that when the injury they had done their brother was firft committed, and the fact was frefh upon their minds, and moft likely to have filled them with a fenfe of guilt, we find no acknowledgment or complaint to one another of fuch a load, as one might imagine it had laid upon them ; and from that event, through a long courfe of years to the time they had gone down

down to Egypt, we read not once of any forrow or compunction of heart, which they had felt during all that time, for what they had done. They had artfully impofed upon their parent---(and as men are ingenious cafuifts in their own af-fairs,) they had, probably, as art-fully impofed upon their own con-fciences;------and poffibly had never impartially reflected upon the action, or confidered it in its juft light, till the many acts of their brother's love and kindnefs had brought it before them, with all the circumftances of aggravation which his behaviour would naturally give it.——They then began maturely to confider what they had done,------that they had firft undefervedly hated him in his childhood for that, which if it was a ground of complaint, ought rather

to have been charged upon the indiscretion of the parent than confidered as a fault in him.   That upon a more just examination and a
better knowledge of their brother,
they had wanted even that pretence.
-------It was not a blind partiality
which seemed first to have directed
their father's affection to him,---
though then they thought so,---for
doubtless so much goodness and be-
nevolence as shone forth in his nature, now that he was a man, could
not lay all of it so deep concealed in
his youth, but the sagacity of a parent's eye would discover it, and that
in course their enmity towards him
was founded upon that which ought
to have won their esteem.---That if
he had incautiously added envy to
their ill will in reporting his dreams,
which presaged his future greatness,

it

it was but the indiscretion of a youth unpractised in the world, who had not yet found out the art of dissembling his hopes and expectations, and was scarce arrived at an age to com prehend there was such a thing in the world as envy and ambition:——that if such offences in a brother, so fairly carried their own excuses with them, what could they say for themselves, when they considered it was for this they had almost unanimously conspired to rob him of his life; —and though they were happily restrained from shedding his blood upon Reuben's remonstrance, that they had nevertheless all the guilt of the intention to answer for. That whatever motive it was, which then stayed their hands, their consciences told them, it could not be a good one, since they had changed the sentence

F 4   for

for one no lefs cruel in itfelf, and
what to an ingenuous nature was
worfe than death, to be fold for a
flave.---The one was common to all,
-------the other only to the unfortunate. That it was not compaffion
which then took place, for had there
been any way open to that, his tears
and entreaties muft have found it,
when they faw the anguifh of his
foul, when he befought and they
would not hear.——That if aught ftill
could heighten the remorfe of ba-
nifhing a youth without provocation,
for ever from his country, and the
protection of his parent, to be expo-
fed naked to the buffetings of the
world, and the rough hand of fome
mercilefs mafter, they would find it
in this reflection, " That the many
afflictions and hardfhips, which they
might naturally have expected would

overtake

overtake the lad, confequent upon this action, had actually fallen upon him."

THAT befides the anguifh of fufpected virtue, he had felt that of a prifon, where he had long lain neglected in a friendlefs condition, and where the affliction of it was rendered ftill fharper by the daily expectation of being remembered by Pharaoh's chief butler, and the difappointment of finding himfelf ungratefully forgotten.------And though Mofes tells us, that he found favour in the fight of the keeper of the prifon, yet the Pfalmift acquaints us that his fufferings were ftill grievous; ---*That his feet were hurt with fetters, and the iron entered even into his foul.* And no doubt, his brethren thought the fenfe of their injury muft

F 5   have

have entered at the fame time, and was then rivetted and fixed in his mind for ever.

It is natural to imagine they argued and reflected in this manner, and there feems no neceffity of feeking for the reafon of their uneafinefs and diftruft in Jofeph's conduct, or any other external caufe, fince the inward workings of their own minds will eafily account for the evil they apprehended.------A feries of benefits and kindneffes from the man they had injured, gradually heightened the idea of their own guilt, till at length they could not conceive, how the trefpafs could be forgiven them;------it appeared with fuch frefh circumftances of aggravation, that though they were convinced his refentment flept, yet they thought it

only

only flept, and was likely fome time or other to awake, and moft probably then, that their father was dead, when the confideration of involving him in his revenge hath ceafed, and all the duty and compaffion he owed to the grey hairs and happinefs of a parent was difcharged, and buried with him.

THIS they exprefs in the confultation held amongft themfelves in the words of the text; and in the following verfe, we find them accordingly fending to him to deprecate the evil they dreaded; and either, becaufe they thought their father's name more powerful than their own, in this application—or rather, that they might not commit a frefh injury in feeming to fufpect his fincerity, they pretend their father's

direction;

direction; for we read they fent mef-
fengers unto Jofeph, faying, Thy father did command before he died
faying,---fo fhall ye fay unto Jofeph,
------" Forgive I pray thee now the
trefpafs of thy brethren and their fin,
for they did unto thee evil: and now
we pray thee, forgive the trefpafs
of the fervants of the God of thy
father." The addrefs was not without art, and was conceived in fuch
words as feemed to fuggeft an argument in their favour,---as if it would
not become him, who was but a fel-
low fervant of their father's God, to
harbour revenge, or ufe the power
their father's God had given him a-
gainft his children.   Nor was there
a reafon in any thing, but the fears
of a guilty confcience to apprehend
it, as appears from the reception
which the addrefs met, which was
                              fuch

fuch as befpoke an uncommon goodnefs of nature; for when they thus
fpake unto him,------the hiftorian
fays, he wept. Sympathy, for the
forrow and diftrefs of fo many fons
of his father, now all in his power,
---pain at fo open and ingenuous a
confeffion of their guilt,---concern
and pity for the long punifhment
they muft have endured by fo ftub-
born a remorfe, which fo many years
feemed not to have diminifhed. The
affecting idea of their condition,
which had feemed to reduce them to
the neceffity of holding up their hands
for mercy, when they had loft their
protector,---fo many tender paffions
ftruggling together at once overcame
him;---he burft into tears, which
fpoke what no language could attempt. It will be needlefs therefore
to enlarge any further upon this incident,

cident, which furnifhes us with fo beautiful a picture of a compaffion-ate and forgiving temper, that I think no words can heighten it,---- but rather let us endeavour to find out by what helps and reafoning, the patriarch might be fuppofed to attain to fo exalted and engaging a virtue. Perhaps you will fay, " That one fo thoroughly convin-ced, as Jofeph feemed to be, of the over-ruling providence of God, which fo evidently made ufe of the malice and paffions of men, and turns them as inftruments in his hands to work his own righteoufnefs and bring a-bout his eternal decrees,---and of which his own hiftory was fo plain an inftance, could not have far to feek for an argument to forgivenefs, or feel much ftruggle in ftifling an inclination againft it.- ----But let any

man

man lay his hand upon his heart and fay, how often, in inftances where anger and revenge had feized him, has this doctrine come in to his aid. ------In the bitternefs of an affront, how often has it calmed his paffions, and checked the fury of his refentment?---True and univerfally believed as the doctrine is amongft us, it feldom does this fervice, though fo well fuited for it, and like fome wife ftatute, never executed or thought of, though in full force, lies as unheeded as if it was not in being.

'Tis plain 'twas otherwife in the prefent inftance, where Jofeph feems to acknowledge the influence it had upon him, in his declaration,--- " *That* it was not they, but God who fent him." And does not this virtue fhine the brighteft in fuch a

pious

pious application of the perfuasion to fo benevolent a purpofe?

WITHOUT derogating from the merit of his forbearance, he might be fuppofed to have caft an eye upon the change and uncertainty of human affairs which he had feen himfelf, and which had convinced him we were all in another's power by turns, and ftand in need of one another's pity and compaffion :----and that to reftrain the cruelties, and ftop the infolences of men's refentments, God has fo ordered it in the courfe of his providence, that very often in this world—our revenges return upon our own heads, and men's violent dealings upon their own pates.

THAT befides thefe confiderations,
that

———that in generoufly forgiving an
enemy ; he was the trueft friend to
his own character, and fhould gain
more to it by fuch an inftance of fub-
duing his fpirit, than if he had taken
a city.------The brave know only how
to forgive ;———it is the moft refined
and generous pitch of virtue, human nature can arrive at.——* Cowards
have done good and kind actions,——
cowards have even fought—nay
fometimes even conquered;———but
a coward never forgave.——It is not
in his nature;———the power of doing it flows only from a ftrength
and greatnefs of foul, confcious of
its own force and fecurity, and a-
bove the little temptations of refent-
ing every fruitlefs attempt to interrupt its happinefs. Moreover, fetting afide all confiderations of his
character,

* Chriftian Hero

character, in paffing by an injury, he was the trueft friend likewife to his own happinefs and peace of mind; he never felt that fretful ftorm of paffions, which hurry men on to acts of revenge, or fuffered thofe pangs or horror which purfue it.—Thus he might poffibly argue, and no further;—for want of a better foundation and better helps, he could raife the building no higher;——to carry it upwards to its perfection, we muft call in to our aid that more fpiritual and refined doctrine introduced upon it by Chrift; namely, to forgive a brother, not only to feven times, but to feventy times feven——that is, without limitation.

In this, the excellency of the gofpel is faid by fome one, to appear with a remarkable advantage; "That

" That a Chriftian is as much difpofed to love and ferve you, when
your enemy, as the mere moral man
can be, when he is your friend."----
This, no doubt, is the tendency of
his religion—but how often, or in
what degrees it fucceeds,——how
nearly the practice keeps pace with
the theory, the all-wife Searcher into the hearts of men, alone is able
to determine.　But it is to be feared, that fuch great effects are not fo
fenfibly felt, as a fpeculative man
would expect from fuch powerful
motives; and there is many a Chriftian fociety, which would be glad
to compound amongft themfelves for
fome leffer degrees of perfection on
one hand, were they fure to be ex-
empted on the other, from the bad
effects of thofe fretful paffions which
are ever taking, as well as ever giving

ving the occasions of strife; the beginnings of which, Solomon aptly compares to the letting out of waters, the opening a breach which no one can be sure to stop, till it has proceeded to the most fatal events.

WITH justice therefore might the son of Sirach conclude, concerning pride, that secret stream, which administers to the overflowings of resentments, that it was not made for man, nor furious anger for him that is born of a woman. That the one did not become his station, and that the other was destructive to all the happiness he was intended to receive from it. How miserably then must those men turn tyrants against themselves, as well as others, who grow splenetic and revengeful not only upon the little unavoidable oppositions
tions

tions and offences they muft meet
with, in the commerce of the world.;
but upon thofe which only reach
them by report, and accordingly tor-
ment their little fouls with medita-
ting how to return the injury, before they are certain they have received one? Whether this eager fen-
fibility of wrongs and refentment a-
rifes from that general caufe, to which
the fon of Sirach feems to reduce all
fierce anger and paffion; or whether
to a certain forenefs of temper, which
ftands in every body's way, and
therefore fubject to be often hurt.
From which ever caufe the diforder
fprings, the advice of the author of
the book of Ecclefiafticus is proper:
" Admonifh a friend, fays he, it
may be he hath not done it; and if
he have, that he do it not again.
Admonifh thy friend, it may be he
hath

hath not faid it ; and if he have, that he fpeak it not again. There is that flippeth in his fpeech, but not from the heart : and who is he, who hath not offended with his tongue ?"

I CANNOT help taking notice here of a certain fpecies of forgivenefs, which is feldom enforced or thought of, and yet is no way below our regard. I mean the forgivenefs of thofe, if we may be allowed the expreffion, whom we have injured ourfelves. One would think that the difficulty of forgiving could only reft on the fide of him, who has received the wrong; but the truth of the fact is often otherwife. The confcioufnefs of having provoked another's refentment, often excites the aggreffor to keep beforehand with the man he has hurt, and not only to

'to hate him for the evil he expects
in return, but even to purſue him
down, and put it out of his power
'to make repriſals.

THE baſeneſs of this is ſuch, that
it is ſufficient to make the ſame obſervation, which was made upon the
crime of parricide amongſt the Gre-
cians:---it was ſo black,——their le-
giſlators did not ſuppoſe it could be
committed, and therefore made no
law to puniſh it.

S E R-

SERMON XIII.

DUTY of setting Bounds to our Desires.

SERMON XIII.

2 KINGS iv. 13.

And he said unto him, Say now unto her, Behold, thou haſt been careful for us with all this care ;—what is to be done for thee?—wouldeſt thou be ſpoken for to the king, or the captain of the hoſt?-----And ſhe anſwered, I dwell among mine own people.

THE firſt part of the text is the words, which the prophet Eliſha puts into the mouth of his ſervant Gehazi, as a meſſage of thanks to the woman of Shunem for her great kindneſs and hoſpitality, of which, after the acknowledgment of his juſt ſenſe, which Gehazi is bid

G 2

to

to deliver in the words ;------" Behold, thou haſt been careful for us
with all this care ;"—he directs him
to enquire, in what manner he may
beſt make a return in diſcharge of
the obligation,— " What ſhall be done
for thee? Wouldeſt thou be ſpoken
for to the king, or the captain of the
hoſt ?"   The laſt part of the text is
the Shunamite's anſwer, which im-
plies a refuſal of the honour or advantage which the prophet intended
to bring upon her, by ſuch an application, which ſhe indirectly ex-
preſſes in her contentment and ſatis-
faction, with what ſhe enjoyed in
her preſent ſtation ; " I dwell amongſt
mine own people." This inſtance
of ſelf-denial in the Shunamite, is
but properly the introduction to her
ſtory, and gives riſe to that long
and very pathetic tranſaction, which
follows

follows in the fupernatural grant of a child, which God had many years denied her.---The affecting lofs of him as foon as he was grown up--- and his reftoration to life by Elifha after he had been fome time dead; the whole of which, though extreme- ly interefting, and from fuch inci- dents as would afford fufficient mat- ter for inftruction, yet as it will not fall within the intention of this dif- courfe, I fhall beg leave at this time barely to confider thefe previous cir- cumftances of it, to which the text confines me, upon which I fhall en- large with fuch reflections as occur, and then proceed to that practical ufe and exhortation, which will na- turally fall from it.

WE find that after Elifha had re- fcued the diftreffed widow and her

two

two fons from the hands of the creditor, by the miraculous multiplication of her oil;---that he paffed on to Shunem, where, we read, was a great woman, and fhe conftrained him to eat bread, and fo it was, that as often as he paffed by, he turned in thither to eat bread. The facred hiftorian fpeaks barely of her temporal condition and ftation in life,--- " That fhe was a great woman," but defcribes not the more material part of her, her virtues and character, becaufe they were more evidently to be difcovered from the tranfaction itfelf, from which it appears, that fhe was not only wealthy, but likewife charitable, and of a very confiderate turn of mind. For after many repeated invitations and entertainments at her houfe, finding his occafions called him to a frequent

paffage

paſſage that way;—ſhe moves her
huſband to ſet up and furniſh a lod-
ging for him, with all the conveni-
encies which the ſimplicity of thoſe
times requiꝛed: " And ſhe ſaid unto her huſband, Behold now I per-
ceive that this is an holy man of
God, which paſſeth by us continually ; let us make him a little cham-
ber I pray thee on the wall, and let
us ſet for him there a bed, and a ta-
ble, and a ſtool, and a candleſtick ;
and it ſhall be when he cometh to
us, that he ſhall turn in thither."----
She perceived he was a holy man,---
ſhe had had many opportunities, as
he paſſed by them continually, of
obſerving his behaviour and deport-
ment, which ſhe had carefully re-
marked, and ſaw plainly what he
was. That the ſanctity and ſimplicity of his manners,---the ſeverity of

his

his life,---his zeal for the religion of his God, and the uncommon fervency of his devotion, when he worshipped before him, which seemed his whole business and employment upon earth;---all bespoke him not a man of this world, but one whose heart and affections were fixed upon another object, which was dearer and more important to him. But as such outward appearances may, and often have been counterfeited, so that the actions of a man are certainly the only interpreters to be relied on, whether such colours are true or false;------so she had heard that all was of a piece there, and that he was throughout consistent: that he had never in any one instance of his life, acted as if he had any views in the affairs of this world, in which he had never interested himself at all,

but

but where the glory of his God, or
the good and prefervation of his fellow-creatures at firft inclined him:
———that in a late inftance before he
came to Shunem, he had done one
of the kindeft and moft charitable actions that a good man could have
done in affifting the widow and fa-
therlefs ;---and as the fact was fingu-
lar, and had juft happened before
her knowledge of him, no doubt fhe
had heard the ftory, with all the tender circumftances which a true report would give it in his favour ;
namely, that a certain woman whofe
hufband was lately dead, and had
left her with her children in a very
helplefs condition------very deftitute
---and what was ftill worfe, charged
with a debt fhe was not able to pay,
---that her creditor bore exceeding
hard upon her, and finding her lit-

tle

tle worth in fubftance, was coming
to take the advantage which the law
allowed of feizing her two fons for
his bondfmen,---fo that fhe had not
only loft her hufband, which had
made her miferable enough already,
but was going to be bereaved of her
children, which were the only comfort and fupport of her life ; that upon her coming to Elifha with this
fad ftory, he was touched with compaffion for her misfortunes, and had
ufed all the power and intereft which
he had with his God to relieve and
befriend her, which in an unheard-
of manner, by the miraculous increafe of her oil, which was the only fubftance fhe had left, he had fo
bountifully effected, as not only to
difintangle her from her difficulties
in paying the debt, but withal, what
was ftill more generous, to enable
her

her to live comfortably the remainder of her days. She considered that charity and compassion was so leading a virtue, and had such an influence upon every other part of a man's character, as to be a sufficient proof by itself of the inward disposition and goodness of the heart, but that so engaging an instance of it as this, exercised in so kind and seasonable a manner, was a demonstration of his,——and that he was in truth what outward circumstances bespoke, a holy man of God.——As the Shunamite's principle and motive for her hospitality to Elisha was just, as it sprung from an idea of the worth and merit of her guest, so likewise was the manner of doing it kind and considerate. It is observable she does not solicit her husband to assign him an apartment in her

own

own houfe, but to build him a cham-
ber in the wall apart;————fhe confidered,————that true piety wanted no
witneffes, and was always moft at
eafe, when moft private ;——that the
tumult and diftraction of a large family were not fit for the filent me-
ditations of fo holy a man, who would
perpetually there meet with fomething either to interrupt his devotion, or offend the purity of his manners;————that moreover, under fuch
an independent roof, where he could
take fhelter as often as his occafions
required, fhe thought he might tafte
the pleafure which was natural to
man, in poffeffing fomething like
what he could call his own,————and
what is no fmall part of conferring
a favour, he would fcarce feel the
weight of it, or at leaft much fel-
domer in this manner, than where

a

a daily invitation and repetition of the kindnefs perpetually put him in mind of his obligation. If any thing could ftill add to this—it was—that it did not appear to be the dry offer of a faint civility, but that it came directly from the heart. There is a nicety in honeft minds, which *will* not accept of a cold and fufpected offer,——and even when it appears to be fincere and truly meant, there is a modefty in true merit which knows not how to accept it ; and no doubt fhe had one, if not both thefe difficulties to conquer in their turns. —For we read, that fhe conftrained him, and in all likelihood forced his acceptance of it with all the warmth and friendly opennefs of a humane and hofpitable temper.

It is with benefits as with injuries
in

in this refpect, that we do not fo much weigh the accidental good or evil they do us, as that which they were defigned to do us.------That is, we confider no part of them fo much as their intention ; and the prophet's behaviour confequent upon this, fhews he beheld it through this medium, or in fome fuch advantageous light as I have placed it.

THERE is no burden fo heavy to a grateful mind, as a debt of kindnefs unpaid ;------and we may believe Elifha felt it fo, from the earneft defire which he had upon the immediate receipt of this, to difcharge himfelf of it, which he expreffes in the text in the warmeft manner ;——" Behold, thou haft been careful for us with all this care: ——What fhall be done for thee ?
Wouldeft

Wouldeſt thou be ſpoken for to the king, or the captain of his hoſt?"--- There is a degree of honeſt impati-ence in the words, ſuch as was na-tuial to a good man, who would not be behind-hand with his benefactoi. ---But there is one thing which may ſeem ſtrange at firſt ſight, that as her ſtation and condition in life was ſuch, that ſhe appeared rather to have a-bounded already than ſtood in want of any thing in this woild which ſuch an application could ſupply,--- why the prophet ſhould not rather have propoſed ſome ſpiritual advan-tage, which, as it would better have become the ſanctity of his character on the one hand, ſo, on the other, it would have done a more real and laſting ſervice to his friend.

But we are to reflect, that in re-turning

turning favours, we act differently
from what we do in conferring them :
——in the one cafe we fimply confider what is beft,——in the other,
what is moft acceptable. The reafon is, that we have a right to act
according to our own ideas of what
will do the party moft good in the
cafe where we beftow a favour,——
but where we return one, we lofe
this right, and act according to his
conceptions who has obliged us, and
endeavour to repay in fuch a manner as we think is moft likely to be
accepted in difcharge of the obligation.——So that, though we are not
to imagine Elifha could be wanting
in religious duties, as well as wifhes
to fo hofpitable a friend, we may yet
fuppofe, he was directed here by this
principle of equity,——and that, in
reflecting in what manner he fhould

requite

requite his benefactrefs, he had confidered, that to one of her affluent
condition who had all the reafonable
comforts of an independent life,-----
it there was any paffion yet unfatis-
ficd, it muft certainly be ambition:
that though in general it was an ir-
regular appetite, which, in moft cafes, 'twas dangerous to gratify, yet,
in effect, 'twas only fo far criminal,
as the power which is acquired was
perverted to bad and vicious purpofes, which it was not likely to be
here, from the fpecimen fhe had already given of her difpofition, which
fhewed, that if fhe did wifh for an
increafe of wealth or honour, fhe
wifhed it only, as it would enable
her more generoufly to extend her
arm in kind offices, and increafe the
power as well as the opportunities
of doing good.

IN justice to Elisha's motive, which must have been good, we must suppose, he considered his offer in this light; and what principally led him to propose it, was the great interest which he had with the king of Israel at that time, which he had merited by a signal service; and as he had no views for himself, he thought it could not be employed so well as in establishing the fortune of one, whose virtue might be so safely trusted with it. It was a justifiable prepossession in her favour,------though one, not always to be relied on; for there is many a one who in a moderate station, and with a lesser degree of power, who has behaved with honour and unblemished reputation, and who has even borne the buffetings of adverse fortunes well, and manifested great presence and

strength

strength of mind under it, whom nevertheless a high exaltation has at once overcome, and so entirely changed, as if the party had left not only his virtue, but even himself behind him.

Whether the Shunamite dreaded to make this dangerous experiment of herself,---or, which is more likely, that she had learned to set bounds to her desires, and was too well satisfied with her present condition to be tempted out of it, she declines the offer in the close of the text:---" I *dwell* amongst my own *people*," as if she had said, " The intended kindness is far from being small, but it is not useful to me; I live here, as thou art a witness, in peace, in a contented obscurity;----- not so high as to provoke envy, nor so low as to be trodden down and despised. In this safe and middle state, as I have lived amongst my own people, so let me die out of the reach, both of the cares and glories of the world.——'Tis fit, O holy man of God! that I learn some time or other to set bounds to my desires, and if I cannot fix them now, when I have already more than my wants require, when shall I hope to do it? ------Or how should I expect, that even this increase of honour or fortune would fully satisfy and content my ambition, should I now give way to it?"

So engaging an instance of unaffected moderation and self-denial, deserves well to be considered by the bustlers in this world ;------because, if we are to trust the face and course

of

of things, we fcarce fee any virtue
fo hard to be put in practice, and
which the generality of mankind
feem fo unwilling to learn, as this
of knowing when they have enough,
and when it is time to give over their
worldly purfuits.------Aye! but nothing is more eafy, you will anfwer,
than to fix this point, and fet certain bounds to it.------" For my own
part, you will fay, I declare, I want
and would wifh no more, but a fufficient competency of thofe things,
which are requifite to the real ufes
and occafions of life, fuitable to the
way I have been taught to expect
from ufe and education."---But re-
collect how feldom it ever happens,
when thefe points are fecured, but
that new occafions and new neceffi-
ties prefent themfelves, and every
day as you grow richer, frefh wants
are

are difcovered, which rife up before you, as you afcend the hill, fo that every ftep you take,------every acceffion to your fortune, fets your defires one degree further from reft and fatisfaction,----- that fomething you have not yet grafped, and poffibly never fhall,------that devil of a phantom unpoffeffed and unpoffeffable, is perpetually haunting you, and ftepping in betwixt you and your contentment.------Unhappy creature! to think of enjoying that bleffing without moderation!---or imagine that fo facred a temple can be raifed upon the foundation of wealth or power!------If the ground-work is not laid within your own mind, they will as foon add a cubit to your ftature, as to your happinefs.------To be convinced it is fo,---pray look up to thofe who have got as high as their warmeft wifhes could carry them in this afcent,---do you obferve they live the better, the longer, the merrier,---or that they fleep the founder in their beds, for having twice as much as they wanted, or well know how to difpofe of?-----Of all rules for calculating happinefs, this is the moft deceitful, and which few but weak minds, and thofe unpractifed in the world too, ever think of applying as the meafure in fuch an eftimation. ------Great, and inexpreffible may be the happinefs, which a moderate fortune and moderate defires with a confcioufnefs of virtue will fecure.---Many are the filent pleafures of the honeft peafant, who rifes chearful to his labour;---why fhould they not? ----Look into his houfe, the feat of each man's happinefs; has he not the

fame

fame domeſtic endearments,-----the
fame joy and comfort in his children,
and as flattering hopes of their doing
well, to enliven his hours and glad
his heart, as you could conceive in
the higheſt ſtation?------And I make
no doubt in general, but if the true
ſtate of his joy and ſufferings, could
be fairly ballanced with thoſe of his
betters, whether any thing would
appear at the foot of the account,
but what would recommend the
moral of this diſcourſe.-----This, I
own, is not to be attained to, by
the cynical ſtale trick of harangu-
ing againſt the goods of fortune,
----they were never intended to be
talked out of the world.------But
as virtue and true wiſdom lie in
the middle of extremes,-------on one
hand, not to neglect and deſpiſe
riches,

riches, so as to forget ourselves, and on the other, not to pursue and love them, so as to forget God;----to have them sometimes in our heads,------but always, something more important in our hearts.

SERMON XIV.

Self-Examination.

SERMON XIV.

ISAIAH i. 3.

The ox knoweth his owner, and the afs his mafter's crib;——but Ifrael doth not know,---my people doth not confider.

'TIS a fevere but an affectionate reproach of the prophet's, laid againft the Ifraelites, which may fafely be applied to every heedlefs, and unthankful people, who are neither won by God's mercies, or terrified by his punifhments.——There is a giddy, thoughtlefs, intemperate fpirit gone forth into the world, which poffeffes the generality of mankind,---and the reafon the world is undone, is, becaufe the world does

H 3　　　　　　　not

not confider,---confiders neither aw-
ful regard to God,---or the true relation themfelves bear to him.---Could
they confider this, and learn to weigh
the caufes, and compare the confe-
quences of things, and to exercife
the reafon, which God has put into us for the government and direction of our lives,---there would be
fome hopes of a reformation:——
but, as the world goes, there is no
leifure for fuch enquiries, and fo full
are our minds of other matters, that
we have not time to afk, or a heart
to anfwer the queftions we ought
to put to ourfelves.

WHATEVER our condition is, 'tis
good to be acquainted with it in
time, to be able to fupply what is
wanting,—and examine the ftate of

our

our accounts, before we come to give them up to an impartial judge.

THE moſt inconſiderate ſee the reaſonableneſs of this,----there being few I believe, either ſo thoughtleſs, or even ſo bad, but that they ſome-times enter upon this duty, and have ſome ſhort intervals of ſelf-examina-tion, which they are forced upon, if from no other motive, yet at leaſt to free themſelves from the load and oppreſſion of ſpirits, they muſt ne-ceſſarily be ſubject to without it.---- But as the ſcripture frequently inti-mates,---and obſervation confirms it daily,------that there are many miſ-takes attending the diſcharge of this duty,---I cannot make the remainder of this diſcourſe more uſeful, than by a ſhort enquiry into them. I ſhall therefore, firſt, beg leave to re-

mind

mind you of fome of the many unhappy ways, by which we often fet
about this irkfome tafk of examining
our works, without being either the
better, or the wifer for the employment.

And firft then let us begin with
that, which is the foundation of almoft all the other falfe meafures we
take in this matter,——that is, the
fetting about the examination of our
works, before we are prepared with
honeft difpofitions to amend them.
---This is beginning the work at the
wrong end. Thefe previous difpofitions in the heart, are the wheels
that fhould make this work go eafily and fuccefsfully forwards,---and
to take them off, and proceed without them, 'tis no miracle, if like
Pharaoh's

Pharaoh's chariots, they that drive them,-----drive them heavily along.

BESIDES, if a man is not sincerely inclined to reform his faults,---'tis not likely he should be inclined to see them,——nor will all the weekly preparations that ever were wrote, bring him nearer the point,—so that with how serious a face soever he begins to examine,——he no longer does the office of an enquirer,—— but an apologift, whose busineſs is not to search for truth,------but skilfully to hide it.------So long---therefore, as this pre-engagement lafts betwixt the man and his old habits, ——there is little profpeȼt of proving his works to any good purpoſe---of whatever kind they are, with ſo ftrong an intereft and power on their ſide.------As in other trials, ſo in this,

H 5 'tis

'tis no wonder, if the evidence is puzzled and confounded, and the several facts and circumstances so twisted from their natural shapes, and the whole proof so altered and confirmed on the other side,——as to leave the last state of that man even worse than the first.

A second unhappy, though general mistake in this great duty of proving our works,---is that which the apostle hints at; in the doing it, not by a direct examination of our own actions, but from a comparative view of them, with the lives and actions of other men.

When a man is going to enter upon this work of self-examination,——there is nothing so common, as to see him——look *round* him——

inftead

inftead of looking *within* him.——IIe looks round,—finds out fome one, who is more malicious,---fees another that is more covetous, a third that is more proud and imperious than himfelf,——and fo indirectly forms a judgment of himfelf, not from a review of his life, and a proving of his own works as the apoftle directs him, but rather from proving the works of others, and from their infirmities and defects drawing a deceitful conclufion in favour of himfelf.----- In all competitions of this kind.---one may venture to fay, there will be ever fo much of felf-love in a man, as to draw a flattering likenefs of one of the parties——and 'tis well ------if he has not fo much malignity too, as to give but a coarfe picture of the other,------finifhed with fo ma--

ny hard ſtrokes, as to make the one as unlike its original as the other.

Thus the Phariſee when he entered the temple,——no ſooner ſaw the publican, but that moment, he formed the idea to himſelf of all the vices and corruptions that could poſſibly enter into the man's character,——and with great dexterity ſtated all his own virtues and good qualities over-againſt them. His abſtinence and frequent faſting,---exactneſs in the debts and ceremonies of the law; not balancing the account as he ought to have done, in this manner:-----What though this man is a publican and a ſinner, have not I my vices as well as he? 'Tis true, his particular office expoſes him to many temptations of committing extortion and injuſtice;---but then---

am

am not I a devourer of widows hou-
fes, and guilty of one of the moft
cruel inftances of the fame crime?
He poffibly is a prophane perfon, and
may fet religion at nought;—but do
not I myfelf for a pretence make long
prayers, and bring the greateft of
all fcandals upon religion, by making
it the cloak to my ambition and
worldly views?—If he, laftly, is de-
bauched or intemperate—am not I
confcious of as corrupt and wanton
difpofitions ; and that a fair and
guarded outfide is my beft pretence
to the oppofite character?

If a man will examine his works
by a comparative view of them with
others ;—this, no doubt, would
be the fairer way, and leaft likely to
miflead him.------But as this is feldom
the method this trial is gone through,

—in fact it generally turns out to be as treacherous and delufive to the man himfelf,——as it is uncandid to the man, who is dragged into the comparifon; and whoever judges of himfelf by this rule,—fo long as there is no fcarcity of vicious characters in the world,—'tis to be feared, he will often take the occafions of triumph and rejoicing,——where in truth, he ought rather to be forry and afhamed.

A THIRD error in the manner of proving our works, is what we are guilty of, when we leave out of the calculation the only material parts of them;—I mean, the motives and firft principles from whence they proceeded. There is many a fair inftance of generofity, chaftity, and felf-denial, which the world may

give

give a man the credit of,—which if he would give himfelf the leifure to reflect upon and trace back to their firft fprings,—he would be confcious, proceeded from fuch views and intentions, as if known, would not be to his honour.——The truth of this may be made evident by a thoufand inftances in life;-----and yet there is nothing more ufual than for a man when he is going upon this duty of felf-examination,---inftead of calling his own ways to remembrance,---to clofe the whole enquiry at once, with this fhort challenge;---" *That he defies the world to fay ill of him.*" If the world has no exprefs evidence, this indeed may be an argument of his good luck;---but no fatisfactory one, of the real goodnefs and innocence of his life.---A man may be a very bad man,—and yet through

caution,

caution,---through deep-laid policy and defign may fo guard all outward appearances, as never to want this negative teftimony on his fide ,---*that the world knows no evil of him*,---how little foever he deferves it.---Of all affays upon a man's felf, this may be faid to be the flighteft ; this method of proving the goodnefs of our works ——differing but little in kind from that unhappy one, which many unwary people take in proving the goodnefs of their coin,---who, if it happens to be fufpicious,---inftead of bringing it either to the balance or the touch-ftone to try its worth,--- they ignorantly go forth ; try, if they can pafs it upon the world ·---if fo, all is well, and they are faved all the expence and pains of enquiring after and detecting the cheat.

A

A FOURTH error in this duty of examination of men's works,---is that of committing the taſk to others ;---an error into which thouſands of well-meaning creatures are inſnared in the Romiſh church by her doctrines of auricular confeſſion, of works of ſupererogation, and the many lucrative practices raiſed upon that capital ſtock.——The trade of which is carried to ſuch a height in Pepiſh countries, that if you was at Rome or Naples now, and was diſpoſed in compliance with the apoſtle's exhortation in the text, to ſet about this duty, to prove your *own* works,------'tis great odds whether you would be ſuffered to do it yourſelf, without interruption ; and you might be ſaid to have eſcaped well, if the firſt perſon you conſulted upon it did not talk you out of your reſolution,

and

and poffibly your fenfes too at the fame time.------Prove your works?---for heaven's fake, defift from fo rafh an undertaking,------what ¹----truft your own fkill and judgment in a matter of fo much difficulty and importance------when there are fo many whofe bufinefs it is,---who underftand it fo well, and who can do it for you with fo much fafety and advantage.

If your works muft be proved, you would be advifed by all means to fend them to undergo this operation with fome one who knows what he is about, either fome expert and noted confeffor of the church,------or to fome convent, or religious fociety, who are in poffeffion of a large ftock of good works of all kinds, wrought up by faints and confeffors,

where

where you may fuit yourfelf—and either get the defects of your own fupplied,—or be accommodated with new ones ready proved to your hands, fealed, and certified to be fo, by the Pope's commiffary and the notaries of his ecclefiaftic court. There needs little more to lay open this fatal error,---than barely to reprefent it. So I fhall only add a fhort remark,—that they who are perfuaded to be thus virtuous by proxy, and will prove the goodnefs of their works only by deputies,—will have no reafon to complain againft God's juftice,—if he fuffers them to go to heaven, only in the fame manner,—that is,—by deputies too.

THE laft miftake which I fhall have time to mention, is that which the methodifts have revived, for 'tis no
new

new error—but one which has mif-
led thoufands before thefe days,
where-ever enthufiafm had got foot-
ing, and that is,——the attempting
to prove their works, by that very
argument which is the greateft proof
of their weaknefs and fupeiftition ;
---I mean that extraordinary impulfe
and intercourfe with the Spiit of
God which they pretend to, and
whofe operations (if you truft them)
are fo fenfibly felt in their hearts and
fouls, as to render at once all other
proofs of their works needlefs to
themfelves.---This, I own, is one of
the moft fummary ways of proceeding in this duty of felf-examination,
and as it proves a man's works in
the grofs, it faves him a world of
fober thought and inquiry after many vexatious particulars.

INDEED,

INDEED, if the premises were true,——the inference is direct. For when a man dreams of these inward workings---and wakes with the impreffion of them ftrong upon his brain; 'tis not ftrange, he fhould think himfelf a chofen veffel,——fanctified within and fealed up unto the perfect day of redemption , and fo long as fuch a one is led captive to this error,---there is nothing in nature to induce him to this duty of examining his own works in the fenfe of the prophet :——for however bad they are,——fo long as his credulity and enthufiafm equal them, 'tis impoffible they fhould difturb his confcience or frighten him into a reformation. Thefe are fome of the unhappy miftakes in the many methods this work is fet about,—which in a great meafure rob us of the fruits we

expected

expected------and sometimes so entirely blaft them, that we are neither the better or wifer for all the
pains we have taken.

THERE are many other falfe fteps,
which lead us the fame way,-----but
the delineation of thefe however may
ferve at prefent, not only as fo many land-marks to guard us from this
dangerous coaft which I have de-
fcribed, but to direct us likewife into that fafe one, where we can only
expect the reward the gofpel promi-
fes. For, if according to the firft
recited caufes, a man fails in examining his works from a difinclina-
tion to reform them,---from partiality of comparifons,---from flattery to
his own motives, and a vain dependence upon the opinion of the
world,——the conclufion is unavoidable,

able,——that he muſt ſearch for the qualities the moſt oppoſite to theſe for his conductors.——And if he hopes to diſcharge this work ſo as to have advantage from it,——that he muſt ſet out upon the principles of an honeſt head, willing to reform itſelf, and attached principally to that object, without regard to the ſpiritual condition of others, or the miſguided opinions which the world may have of himſelf.

THAT for this end,——he muſt call his own ways to remembrance, and ſearch out his ſpirit,——ſearch his actions with the ſame critical ex-actneſs and ſame piercing curioſity, we are wont to ſit in judgment up-on others;——varniſhing nothing ——and diſguiſing nothing. If he proceeds thus, and in every relation

of

of life takes a full view of himfelf without prejudice,------traces his actions to their principles without mercy, and looks into the dark corners and receffes of his heart without fear ——and upon fuch an enquiry—— he acts confiftent with his view in it, by reforming his errors, feparating the drofs and purifying the whole mafs with repentance;------this will bid fair for examining a man's works in the apoftle's fenfe :---and whoever difcharges the duty thus---with a view to fcripture, which is the rule in this cafe------and to reafon, which is the applier of this rule in all cafes------ need not fear but he will have what the prophet calls *rejoicing in himfelf,* and that he will lay the foundation of his peace and comfort where it ought to lie------that is, within him-felf---in the teftimony of a good con-fcience,

ïcience, and the joyful expectation
.that having done his utmoſt to examine his *own* woiks here, that God
will accept them heieafter through
the merits of Chriſt, which God
grant. Amen.

SERMON XV.

JOB's Expoſtulation with his WIFE.

SERMON XV.

JOB xi. 10.

What shall we receive good at the hand of God, and shall we not receive evil also?

THESE are the words of Job uttered in the depth of his misfortunes, by way of reproof to his wife, for the counsel we find she had given him in the foregoing verse; namely, not to retain his integrity any longer,------but to *curse God and die.* Though it is not very evident, what was particularly meant and implied in the words----" Curse God and die,"------yet it is certain from Job's reply to them, that they directed him to some step, which was

I 3

rash

rafh and unwarrantable, and probably, as it is generally explained, meant that he fhould openly call God's juftice to an account, and by a blafphemous accufation of it, provoke God to deftroy his being: as if fhe had faid,------After fo many fad things which have befallen thee, notwithftanding thy integrity, what gaineft thou by ferving God, feeing he bears thus hard upon thee, as though thou waft his enemy?——ought fo faithful a fervant as thou haft been, to receive fo much unkind treatment at his hands;——and tamely to fubmit to it?——patiently to fuftain the evils he has brought upon thy houfe, and neither murmur with thy lips, nor charge him with injuftice?---bear it not thus;---and as thy piety could not at firft protect thee from fuch misfortunes,——nor thy

behaviour

behaviour under them could fince move God to take pity on thee,—change thy conduct towards him,—boldly expoftulate with him,—upbraid him openly with unkindnefs,—call his juftice and providence to an account for oppreffing thee in fo undeferved a manner, and get that benefit by provoking him, which thou haft not been able to obtain by ferving him:—to die at once by his hands, and be freed, at leaft, from the greater mifery of a lingering, and a more tormenting death.

On the other hand, fome interpreters tell us,—that the word *curfe*, in the original, is equivocal, and does more literally fignify here, to blefs, than to blafpheme, and confequently that the whole is rather to be confidered as a farcaftical fcoff at Job's piety —As if it had been said;—Go to,——blefs God,——and die;---fince thou art ready to praife him in troub'es as thou haft done, go on in thy own way, and fee how God will reward thee, by a miferable death which thou canft not avoid.

WITHOUT difputing the merit of thefe two interpretations, it may not feem an improbable conjecture, that the words imply fomething ftill different from what is exprefled in either of them,------and inftead of fuppofing them as an incitement to blafpheme God,——which was madnefs, ——or that they were intended as an infult, which was unnatural,—that her advice to curfe God and die, was meant here, that he fhould refolve upon a voluntary death himfelf, which was an act not only in

his

his own power, but what carried
some appearance of a remedy with it,
and promised, at least at first sight,
some respite from pain, as it would
put an end, both to his life and his
misfortunes together.

One may suppose that with all
the concern and affection which was
natural, she beheld her lord afflicted
both with poverty and sickness,---
by one sudden blow brought down
from his palace to the dunghill.____
In one mournful day, she saw, that
not only the fortunes of his house
were blasted, but likewise the hopes
of his posterity cut off for ever by
the untimely loss of his children.------
She knew he was a virtuous and an
upright man, and deserved a better
fate,——her heart bled the more for
him,—she saw the prospect before

him

him was dreadful,—that there appeared no poffible means, which could retrieve the fad fituation of his affairs,—that death, the laft——the fureft friend to the unfortunate, could only fet him free ;—and that it was better to refolve upon that at once, than vainly endeavour to wade through fuch a fea of troubles, which in the end would overwhelm him. ---We may fuppofe her fpirits finking under thofe apprehenfions, when fhe began to look upon his conftancy as a fruitlefs virtue, and from that perfuafion, to have faid unto him,---Curfe God,---depend no longer upon him, nor wait the iffues of his providence which has already forfaken thee,——as there is no help from that quarter,---refolve to extricate thyfelf---and fince thou haft met with no juftice in this world,---leave it,---

die

die---and force thy paffage into a better country, where misfortunes cannot follow thee.

WHETHER this paraphrafe upon the words is juft, or the former interpretations be admitted,---the reply in the text is equally proper,---What!---fhall we receive good at the hands of God, and fhall we not receive evil alfo? Are not both alike the difpenfations of an all-wife and good Being, who knows and determines what *is beft?* and wherefore fhould I make myfelf the judge, to receive the one, and yet be fo partial as to rejeft the other, when by fairly putting both into the fcale, I may be convinced how much the good outweighs the evil in all cafes? in my own, confider how ftrong this argument is againft me.

I 6

In the beginning of my days, how did God crown me with honour? In how remarkable a manner did his providence fet a hedge about me, and about all that I had on every fide?---how he profpered the works of my hands, fo that our fubftance and happinefs increafed every day?

And now, when for reafons beft known to his infinite wifdom, he has thought fit to try me with afflictions, ---fhall I rebel againft him in finning with my lips, and charging him fool-ifhly?-- ---God forbid.------O rather may I look up towards that hand which has bruifed me,---for he ma-keth fore and he bindeth up,---he woundeth and his hands make whole; from his bounty only has if-fued all I had, from his wifdom,---all I have loft, for he giveth and he

hath

hath taken away,---bleffed be his name.

THERE are few inftances of particular virtue more engaging than thofe
of this heroic caft; and if we may
take the teftimony of a heathen phi-
lofopher upon it, there is not an object in this world which God can be
fuppofed to look down upon with
greater pleafure, than that of a good
man involved in misfortunes, furrounded on all fides with difficulties,
---yet chearfully bearing up his head,
and ftruggling againft them with
firmnefs and conftancy of mind.---
Certainly to our conceptions fuch
objects muft be truly engaging,---and
the reafon of fo exalted an encomium
from this hand, is eafy to be gueffed:
no doubt the wifeft of the heathen
philofophers had found from obfervation upon the life of man, that the
many

many troubles and infirmities of his
nature, the ficknefles, difappointments, forrows for the lofs of children or property, with the number-
lefs other calamities and crofs accidents, to which the life of man is
fubject, were in themfelves fo *great*,
—— and fo *little* folid comfort to be
adminiftered from the mere refine-
ments of philofophy in fuch emergencies, that there was no virtue
which required greater efforts, or
which was found fo difficult to be at-
chieved upon moral principles ;
upon moral principles---which had no
foundation to fuftain this great
weight, which the infirmities of our
nature laid upon it. And for this
reafon 'tis obfervable that there is
no fubject, upon which the moral
writers of antiquity have exhaufted
fo much of their eloquence, or where
they

they have ſpent ſuch time and pains, as in this of endeavouring to reconcile men to theſe evils. Infomuch, that from thence in moſt modern languages, the patient enduring of affliction has by degrees obtained the name of philoſophy, and almoſt monopolized the word to itſelf, as if it was the chief end or compendium of all the wiſdom which philoſophy had to offer. And indeed conſidering what lights they had, ſome of them wrote extremely well; yet, as what they ſaid proceeded more from the head than the heart, 'twas generally more calculated to ſilence a man in his troubles, than to convince, and teach him how to bear them. And therefore however ſubtle and ingenious their arguments might appear in the reading, 'tis to be feared they loſt much of their efficacy

ficacy, when tried in the application.
If a man was thruft back in the
world by difappointments, or------as
was Job's cafe------had fuffered a fudden change in his fortunes, from an
affluent condition was brought down
by a train of cruel accidents, and
pinched with poverty,---philofophy
would come in, and exhort him to
ftand his ground,------it would tell
him that the fame greatnefs and
ftrength of mind, which enabled him
to behave well in the days of his profperity, fhould equally enable him to
behave well in the days of his adverfi-
ty ;---that it was the property of only
weak and bafe fpirits, who were info-
lent in the one, to be dejected and overthrown by the other; whereas great
and generous fouls were at all times
calm and equal.—As they enjoyed the
advantages of life with indifference,----
they

they were able to refign them with the fame temper,—and confequently——were out of the reach of fortune All which, however fine, and likely to fatisfy the fancy of a man at eafe, could convey but little confolation to a heart already pierced with forrow,—nor is it to be conceived how an unfortunate creature fhould any more receive relief from fuch a lecture, however juft, than a man racked with an acute fit of the gout or ftone, could be fuppofed to be fet free from torture, by hearing from his phyfician a nice differtation upon his cafe. The philofophic confolations in ficknefs, or in afflictions for the death of friends and kindred, were juft as efficacious,—and were rather in general to be confidered as good fayings than good remedies. ——So that, if a man was bereaved

. of

of a promifing child, in whom all his hopes and expectations centered ---or a wife was left deftitute to mourn the lofs and protection of a kind and tender hufband, Seneca or Epictetus would tell the penfive parent and difconfolate widow,------ that tears and lamentation for the dead were fruitlefs and abfurd,--- that to die, was the neceffary and unavoidable debt of nature,---and as it could admit of no remedy------'twas impious and foolifh to grieve and fret themfelves upon it. Upon fuch fage counfel, as well as many other leffons of the fame ftamp, the fame reflection might be applied, which is faid to have been made by one of the Roman emperors, to one who adminiftered the fame confolations to him on a like occafion---to whom, advifing him to be comforted, and

make

make himſelf eaſy, ſince the event
had been brought about by a fatality
and could not be helped,-----he re-
plied,——" That this was ſo far from
leſſening his trouble——that it was
the very circumſtance which occa-
ſioned it." So that upon the whole
——when the true value of theſe,
and many more of their current arguments have been weighed and
brought to the teſt—one is led to
doubt, whether the greateſt part of
their heroes, the moſt renowned for
conſtancy, were not much more indebted to good nerves and ſpirits,
or the natural happy frame of their
tempers, for behaving well, than to
any extraordinary helps, which they
could be ſuppoſed to receive from
their inſtructors. And therefore I
ſhould make no ſcruple to aſſert, that
ene ſuch inſtance of patience and re-
ſignation

fignation as this, which the fcripture gives us in the perfon of Job, of one moft pompoufly declaiming upon the contempt of pain and poverty, but of a man funk in the loweft condition of humanity, to behold him when ftripped of his eftate,—his wealth, his friends, his children,—— cheerfully holding up his head, and entertaining his hard fortune with firmnefs and ferenity,——and this, not from a ftoical ftupidity, but a juft fenfe of God's providence, and a perfuafion of his juftice and goodnefs in all his dealings.——Such an example, I fay, as this, is of more univerfal ufe, fpeaks truer to the heart, than all the heroic precepts, which the pedantry of philofophy have to offer.

THIS leads me to the point I aim

at

as in this difcourfe;—— namely, that there are no principles but thofe of religion to be depended on in cafes of real ftrefs, and that thefe are able to encounter the worft emergencies; and to bear us up under all the changes and chances to which our life is fubject.

CONSIDER then what virtue the very firft principle of religion has, and how wonderfully it is conducive to this end. That there is a God, a powerful, a wife and good being, who firft made the world and continues to govern it;---by whofe goodnefs all things are defigned---and by whofe providence all things are conducted to bring about the greateft and beft ends. The forrowful and penfive wretch that was giving way to his misfortunes, and mournfully

finking

finking under them, the moment this doctrine comes in to his aid, hufhes all his complaints---and thus fpeaks comfort to his foul,——" It is the Lord, let him do what feemeth him good,---without his direction I know that no evil can befal me,---without his permiffion that no power can hurt me,---it is impoffible a being fo wife fhould miftake my happinefs——or that a being fo good fhould contradict it. If he has denied me riches or other advantages, ---perhaps he forefees the gratifying my wifhes would undo me, and by my own abufe of them be perverted to my ruin.——If he has denied me the requeft of children,---or in his providence has thought fit to take them from me---how can I fay--- whether he has not dealt kindly with me, and only taken that away which

he

he forefaw would embitter and
fhorten my days.---It does fo, to
thoufands, where the difobedience
of a thanklefs child has brought
down the parents grey hairs with
forrow to the grave. Has he vifited
me with ficknefs, poverty, or other
difappointments?---can I fay, but
thefe are bleflings in difguife?---fo
many different expreflions of his care
and concern to difintangle my
thoughts from this world, and fix
them upon another,---another, a better world beyond this!"------This
thought opens a new fcene of hope
and confolation to the unfortunate;
---and as the perfuafion of a providence reconciles him to the evils he
has fuffered,——this profpect of a future life gives him ftrength to de-
fpife them, and efteem the light afflictions of his life as they are---not
worthy

worthy to be compared to what is referved for him hereafter.

THINGS are great or fmall by comparifon——and he looks no further than this world, and balances the accounts of his joys and fufferings from that confideration, finds all his forrows enlarged, and at the clofe of them will be apt to look back, and caft the fame fad reflection upon the whole, which the patriarch did to Pharaoh,---" That few and evil had been the days of his pilgrimage." But let him lift up his eyes towards heaven, and ftedfaftly behold the life and immortality of a future ftate, ------he then wipes away all tears from off his eyes for ever and ever; ——like the exiled captive, big with the hopes that he is returning home, ——he feels not the weight of his

chains,

chains, or counts the days of his captivity; but looks forward with rapture towards the country where his heart is fled before.

THESE are the aids which religion offers us towards the regulating of our fpirit under the evils of life,——but like great cordials,——they are feldom ufed but on greater occurrences.---In the leffer evils of life we feem to ftand unguarded---and our peace and contentment are overthrown, and our happinefs broke in upon by a little impatience of fpirit, under the crofs and untoward accidents we meet with.————Thefe ftand unprovided for, and we neglect them as we do the flighter indifpofitions of the body——which we think not worth treating ferioufly--- and fo leave them to nature. In good habits of the body, this may do,——and I would gladly believe, there are such good habits of the temper,---such a complexional ease and health of heart, as may often save the patient much medicine.--- We are still to confider---that however such good frames of mind are got---they are worth preserving by all rules;---patience and contentment,---which like the treasure hid in the field for which a man sold all he had to purchase—is of that price that it cannot be had at too great a purchase, since without it, the best condition in life cannot make us happy,——and with it, it is impossible we should be miserable even in the worst.—Give me leave therefore to close this discourse with some reflections upon the subject of a contented mind---and the duty in man

of

of regulating his fpirit, in our way through life;------a fubject in every body's mouth-----preached upon daily to our friends and kindred---but too oft in fuch a ftyle, as to convince the party lectured, only of this truth;—that we bear the misfortunes of others with excellent tranquillity.

I believe there are thoufands fo extravagant in their ideas of contentment, as to imagine that it muft confift in having every thing in this world turn out the way they wifh---that they are to fit down in happinefs, and feel themfelves fo at eafe at all points, as to defire nothing better and nothing more. I own there are inftances of fome, who feem to pafs through the world, as if all their paths had been ftrewed with rofe-buds of delight;---but a little ex

perience

perience will convince us, 'tis a fatal expectation to go upon.——We are born to trouble; and we may depend upon it whilft we live in this world we fhall have it, though with intermiffions---that is, in whatever ftate we are, we fhall find a mixture of good and evil; and therefore the true way to contentment, is to know to receive thefe certain viciffitudes of life,---the returns of good and evil, fo as neither to be exalted by the one, or overthrown by the other, but to bear ourfelves towards every thing which happens with fuch eafe and indifference of mind, as to hazard as little as may be. This is the true temperate climate fitted for us by nature, and in which every wife man would wifh to live.---God knows, we are perpetually ftraying out of it, and by giving wings to our imagi-

nations

nations in the tranſports we dream of, from ſuch or ſuch a ſituation in life, we are carried away alternately into all the extremes of hot and cold, for which as we are neither fitted by nature, or prepared by expectation, we feel them with all their violence, and with all their danger too.

GOD, for wiſe reaſons, has made our affairs in this world, almoſt as fickle and capricious as ourſelves.---Pain and pleaſure, like light and darkneſs, ſucceed each other; and he that knows how to accommodate himſelf to their periodical returns, and can wiſely extract the good from the evil,---knows only how to live;---this is true contentment, at leaſt all that is to be had of it in this-world, and for this every man muſt be indebted not to his fortune but to himſelf.---

And

And indeed it would have been ftrange, if a duty fo becoming us as independent creatures---and fo necef-fary befides to all our well-beings, had been placed out of the reach of any in fome meafure to put in practice------and for this reafon, there is fcarce any lot fo low, but there is fomething in it to fatisfy the man whom it has befallen ; providence having fo ordered things, that in every man's cup, how bitter foever, there are fome cordial drops------fome good circumftances, which if wifely extracted are fufficient for the purpofe he wants them,------that is, to make him contented, and if not happy, at leaft refigned. May God blefs us all with this fpirit, for the fake of Jefus Chrift, Amen.

THE END.

Breinigsville, PA USA
24 March 2011
258282BV00004B/49/P

9 781171 088011